BUDDHIST IMAGES

by Taikichi Irie
&
Shigeru Aoyama

translated by

Thomas I. Elliott

HOIKUSHA
保育社

THE HEART AND ENVIRONS OF NARA

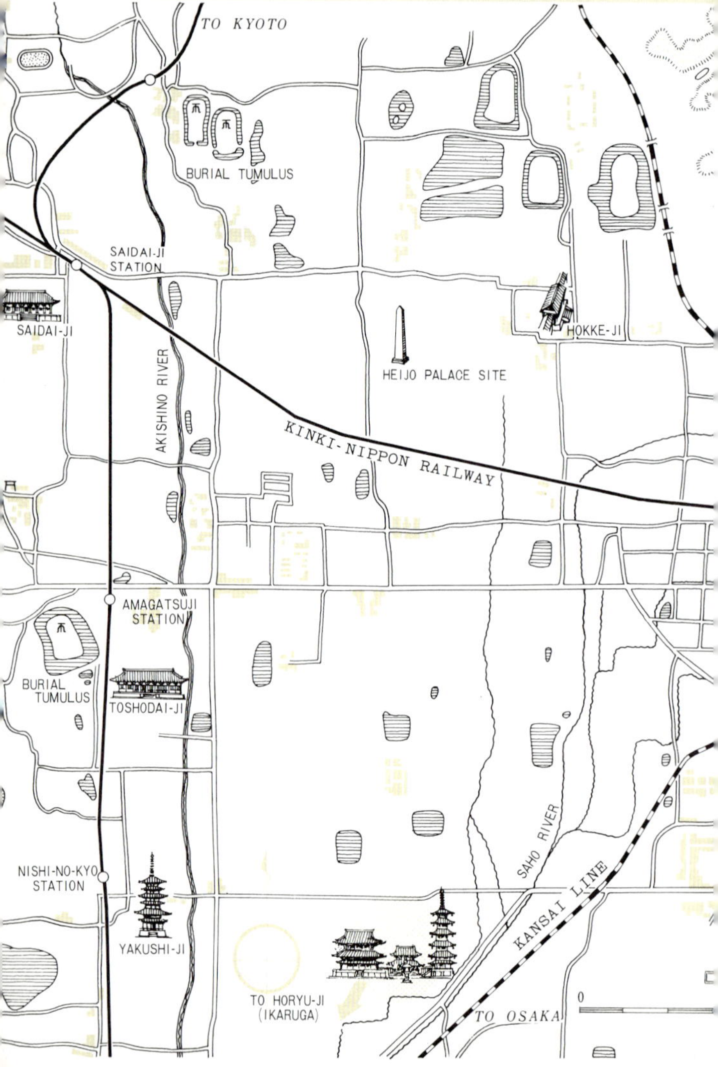

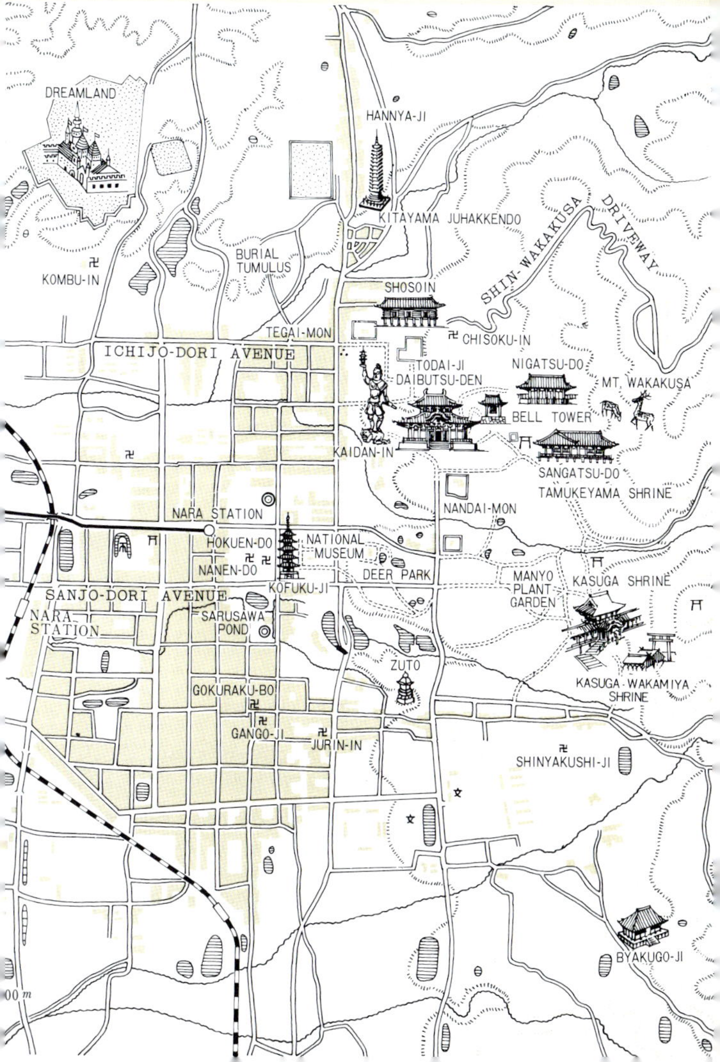

DREAMLAND
HANNYA-JI
KITAYAMA JUHAKKENDO
SHIN-WAKAKUSA DRIVEWAY
BURIAL TUMULUS
KOMBU-IN
SHOSOIN
TEGAI-MON
CHISOKU-IN
ICHIJO-DORI AVENUE
TODAI-JI DAIBUTSU-DEN
NIGATSU-DO
MT. WAKAKUSA
BELL TOWER
KAIDAN-IN
SANGATSU-DO
TAMUKEYAMA SHRINE
NANDAI-MON
NARA STATION
HOKUEN-DO
NATIONAL MUSEUM
NANEN-DO
DEER PARK
MANYO PLANT GARDEN
KASUGA SHRINE
KOFUKU-JI
SANJO-DORI AVENUE
NARA STATION
SARUSAWA POND
ZUTO
KASUGA-WAKAMIYA SHRINE
GOKURAKU-BO
GANGO-JI
JURIN-IN
SHINYAKUSHI-JI
BYAKUGO-JI
00 m

Contents

Shaka Nyorai	1	Amida Nyorai	9
Yakushi Nyorai	16	Dainichi Nyorai	23
Miroku Bosatsu	27	Kannon Bosatsu	32
Monju and Fugen	53	Nikko and Gakko	56
Jizo Bosatsu	62	Kokuzo Bosatsu	65
Myoo	68	Shitenno	72

Bon Ten and Taishaku Ten 80

Kongo Rikishi	84	Juni Jinsho	88
Tennyo	92		

Viewing Buddhist Images 98
Beginnings of Buddhist Art in Japan 100
Buddhist Images – Their Attributes and Figures 104
Materials and Techniques 113
Buddhist Images: Shape and *Kokoro* 121
Glossary 133

BUDDHIST IMAGES

by Taikichi Irie & Shigeru Aoyama
translated by Thomas I. Elliott

No.18 of Hoikusha's Color Books Series.Published by Hoikusha Publishing Co., Ltd., 8-6, 4-chome, Tsurumi, Tsurumi-ku, Osaka,538 Japan. ISBN 4-586-54018-4. First Edition in 1970. 10th Edition in 1990. Printed in JAPAN

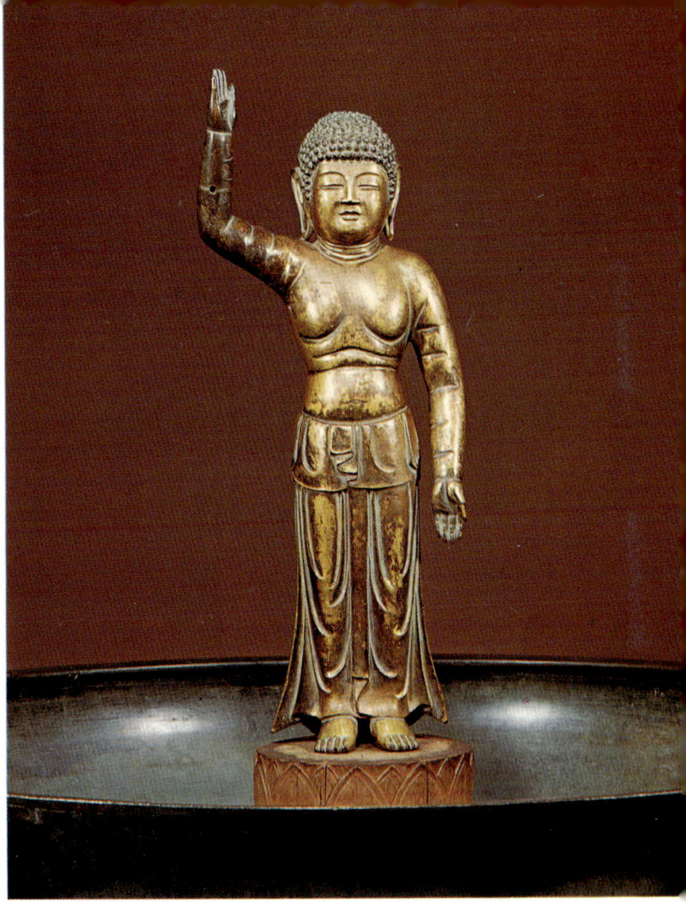

1. Tanjo Shaka (Buddha at birth); Todai-ji Temple, Nara Period, Bronze, 46.9 cm

Shaka Nyorai

Taken strictly, the Japanese word *butsuzo* refers to images of buddhas, i.e., *hotoke, butsuda* and *nyorai.* Popular reference, however, also includes Jizo, Kannon, and other bodhisattvas, and buddha guardians or attendants like Myoo, Ten, and Juni Jinsho. People even refer to statues of famous priests like Kukai (Kobo Daishi) and Ganjin as *butsuzo.* Its usage today thus suggests that *butsuzo* is an abbreviated reference to all Buddhism-related, sculptured images. Indeed, the term occasionally extends to include painted images.

With the word *butsuzo* including so many statues and paintings, it is hardly surprising that the layman experiences difficulty in understanding and appreciating Buddhist images. In fact, lovers of the fine arts, and so-called experts in Buddhist sculpture, do not always properly distinguish even the important categories *nyorai* and *bosatsu.* To understand a religious art like *butsuzo*, one must let artistic appreciation wait, and first acquire a basic historical background and study the over-all iconographical classification of Buddhist images.

The four broad *butsuzo* categories are Nyorai, Bosatsu, Myoo, and Ten. Nyorai is the basic *butsuzo*, originally synonymous with *butsuda*, a title reserved for men who gained enlightenment. The first man to gain enlightenment was Sakyamuni (Gautama Siddhartha 563BC.?–483BC.?)–Shaka, in Japanese – the founder of Buddhism. The primary *butsuzo*, therefore, is Shaka. Sakyamuni was a man among men. Although physically and spiritually superior to all men, he chose to live an austere and ascetic life. His figure is the basis for all Nyorai (Butsuda, Shaka) images.

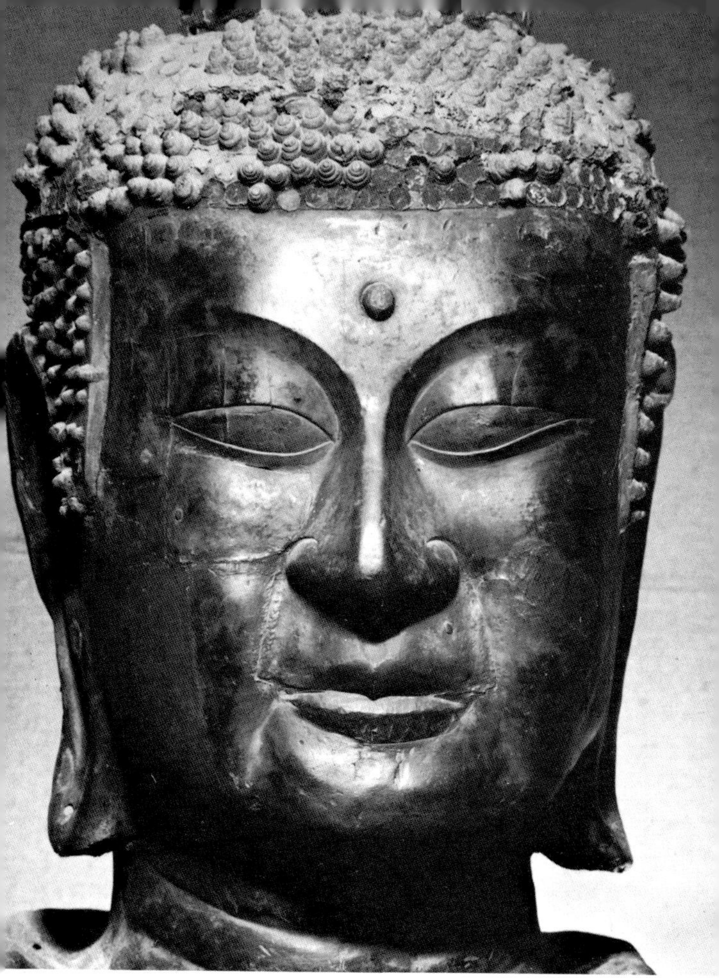

2. **Shaka Nyorai, seated;** the Asuka Daibutsu, Ango-in Temple (Asuka-ji Temple), Asuka Period, Bronze, 275.7 cm

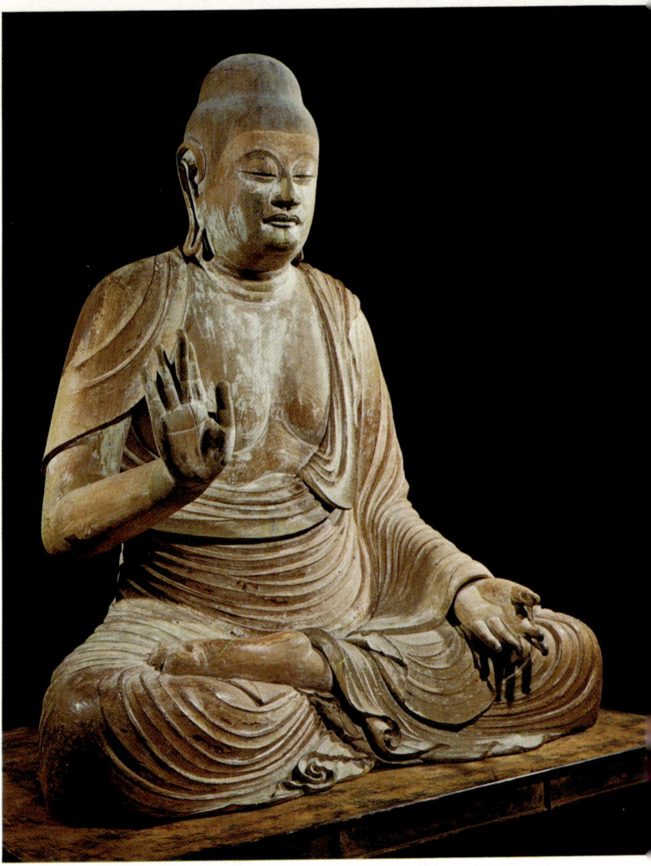

3. **Shaka Nyorai, seated;** Mirokudo Hall, Muro-ji Temple, early Heian Period, Wood, 105.7 cm

4. **Shaka Nyorai, with two attendants;** Kondo Hall, Horyu-ji Temple, Asuka Period, Bronze, 86.3 cm

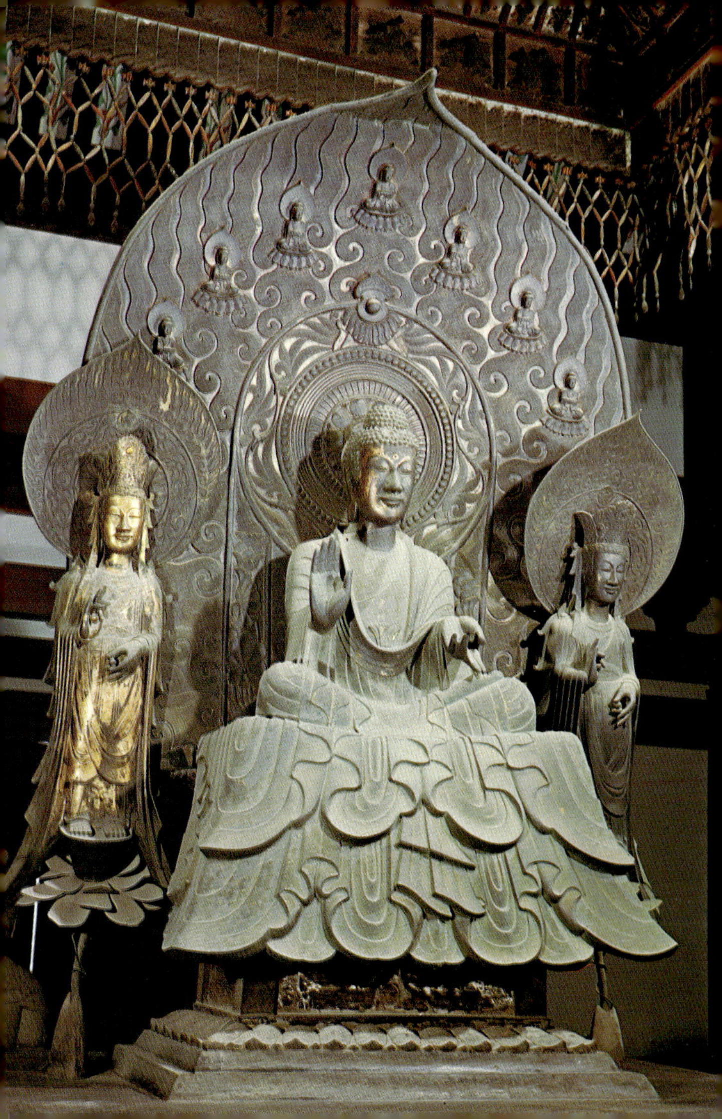

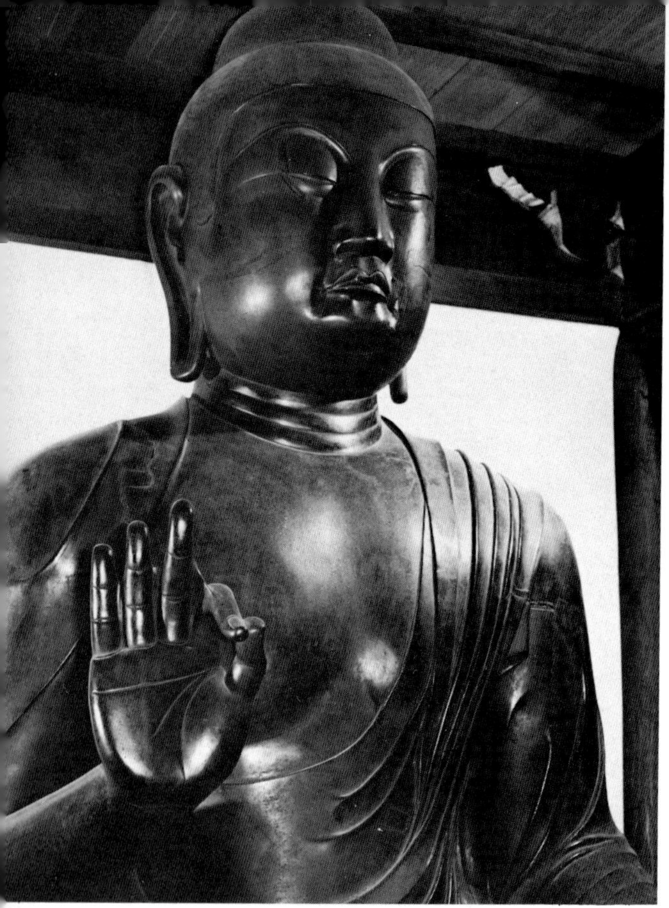

5. **Shaka Nyorai, seated;** Kaniman-ji Temple, early Nara Period, Bronze, 262 cm

6. **Shaka Nyorai, standing** (Seiryo-ji-style Shaka); Main Hall, Saidai-ji Temple, Kamakura Period, Wood, 168 cm

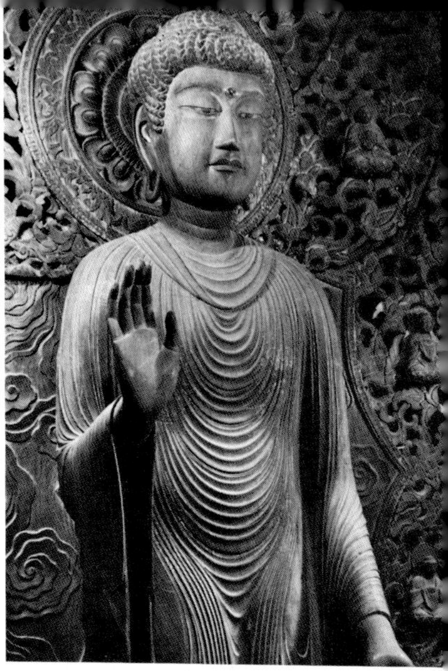

7. **Shaka Nehan** (Buddha about to enter nirvana); north wall, first level of Horyu-ji Temple's five-storied pagoda, Nara Period, Stucco

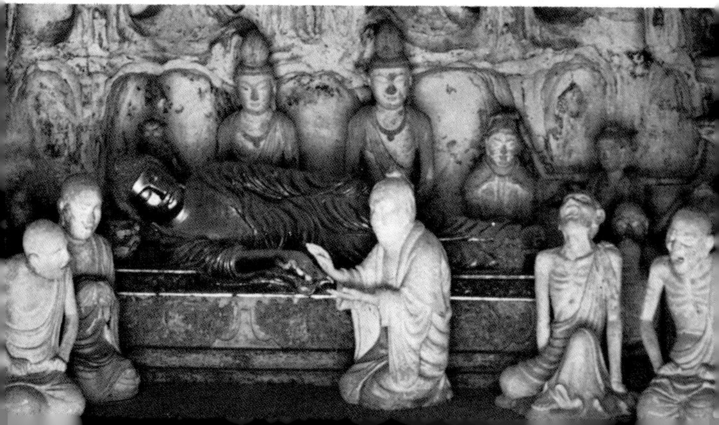

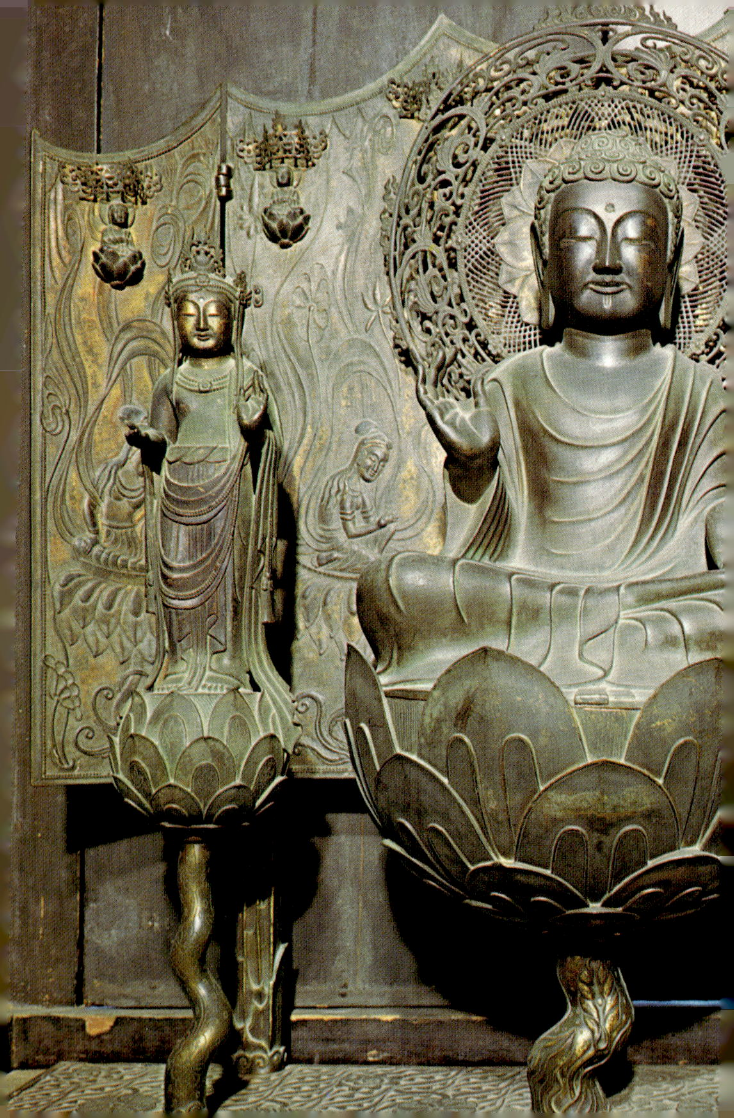

Amida Nyorai

Amida Nyorai is one of the most popular Buddhist deities in Japan. He made forty-eight promises to man, the eighth of which says that he who sincerely beseeches Amida by name will be received at death and guided to the Pure Land, millions of miles off in the Western Paradise, there to pursue under ideal conditions the quest for ultimate perfection. Thus through simple prayer to Amida, common man was given a way to enter nirvana. Amida Nyorai appears with thirty-two attributes and eighty secondary characteristics, the same as Shaka.

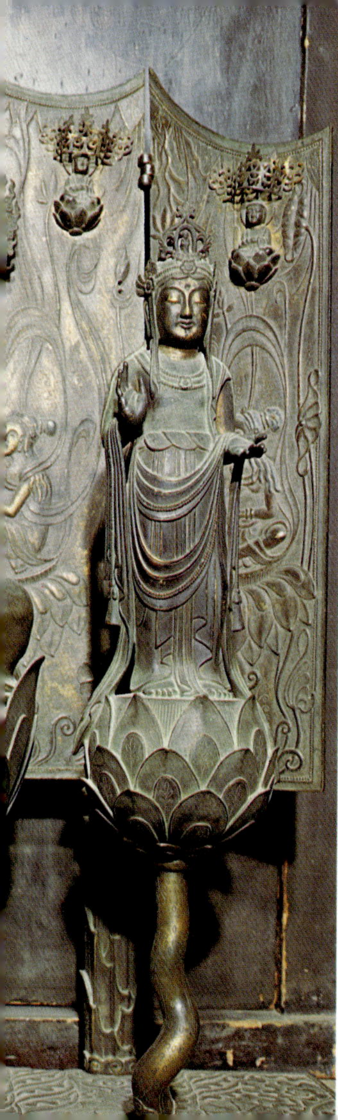

8. **Amida Nyorai, seated, and attendants;** Hozoden Treasury, Horyu-ji Temple, Hakuho Period, Bronze, 33.3 cm, attendants 27 cm

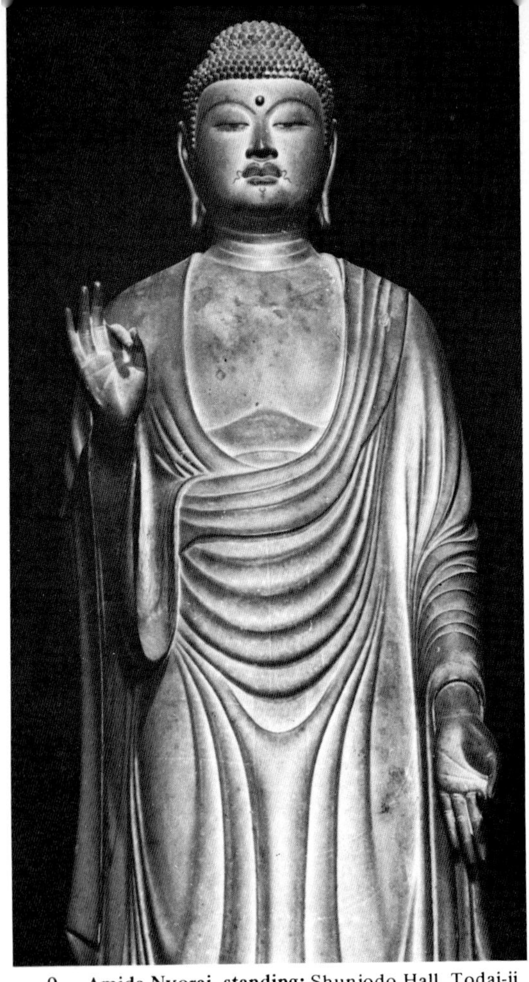

9. **Amida Nyorai, standing;** Shunjodo Hall, Todai-ji Temple, Kamakura Period, Wood, 98.5 cm

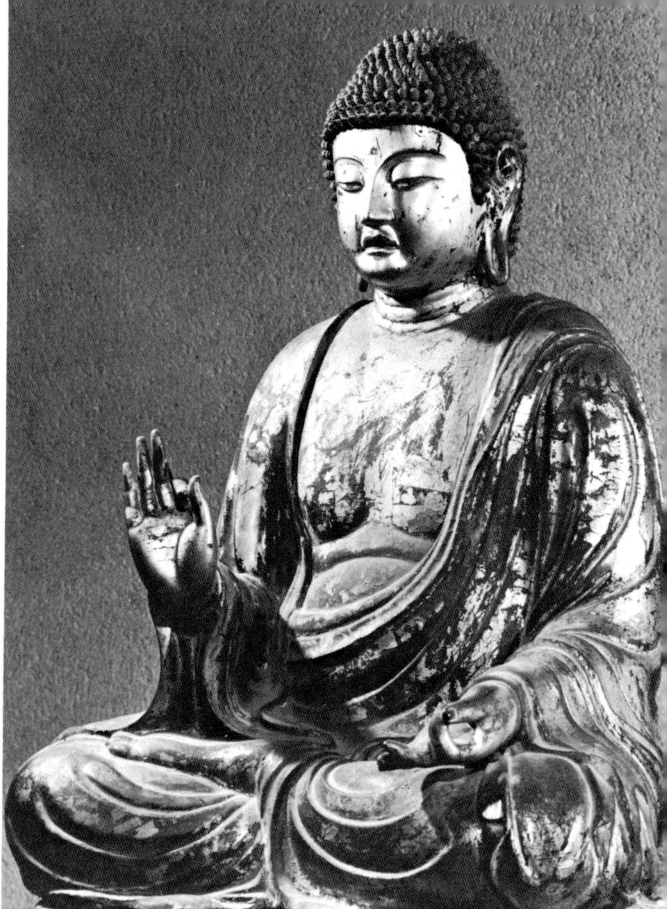

10. Amida Nyorai, seated; one of four images in Saidai-ji Temple's Pagoda, Nara Period, Wood, 69.4 cm

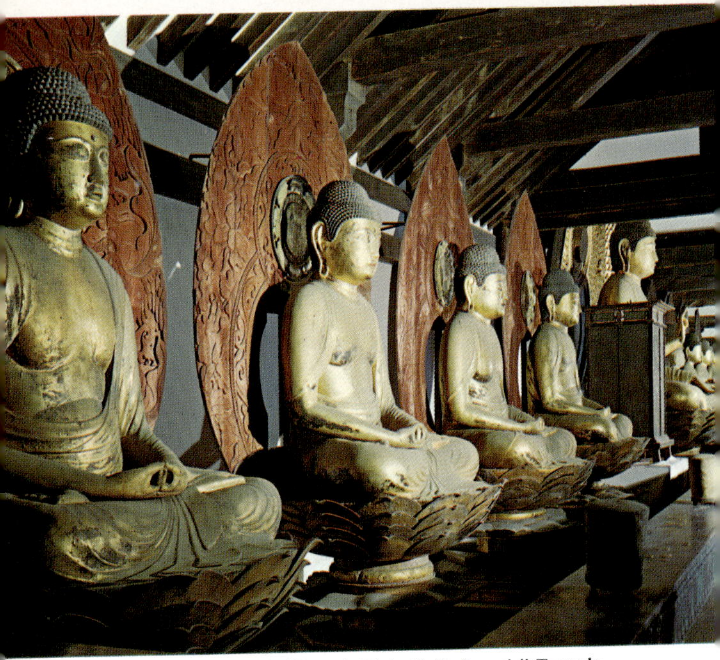

11. Nine seated Amida Nyorai; Main Hall, Joruri-ji Temple, late Heian Period, Wood, central Amida 244 cm, others 138.7 – 145.4 cm

Each living soul fits into one of nine categories of spiritual commitment and attainment, called the nine classes of nirvana. The particular category, or level, determines the way an individual passes to the Pure Land. There are also nine Amida manifestations, one assigned to receive souls into each class of nirvana. During the Fujiwara Period (950–1170), it was faddish to group all nine Amida Nyorai images in one hall.

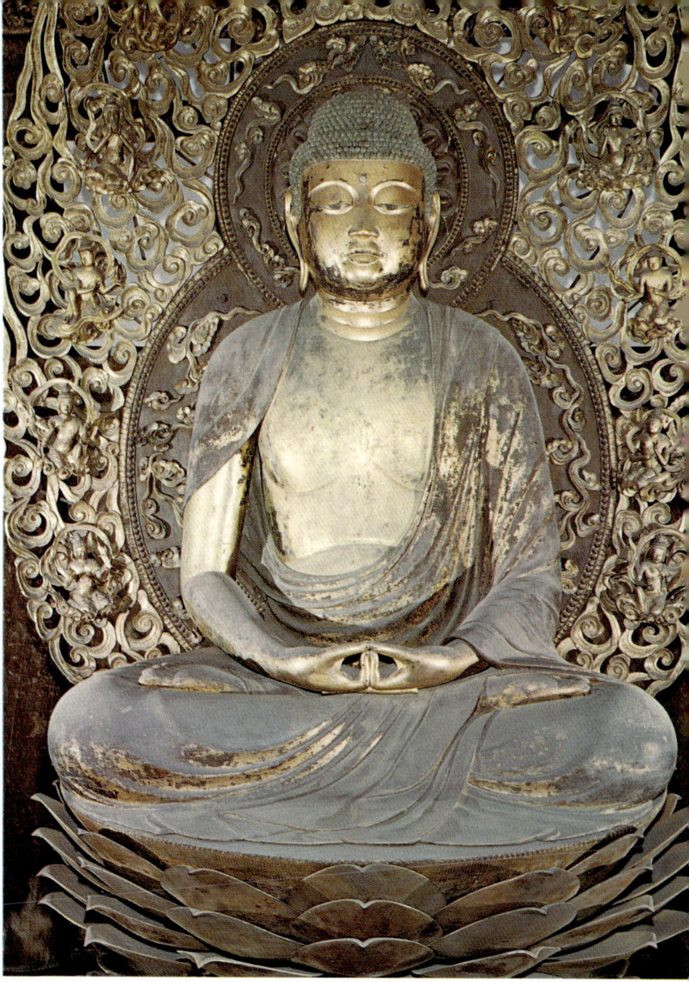

12. Amida Nyorai, seated; Phoenix Hall, Byodo-in Temple, late Heian Period, Wood, 306 cm

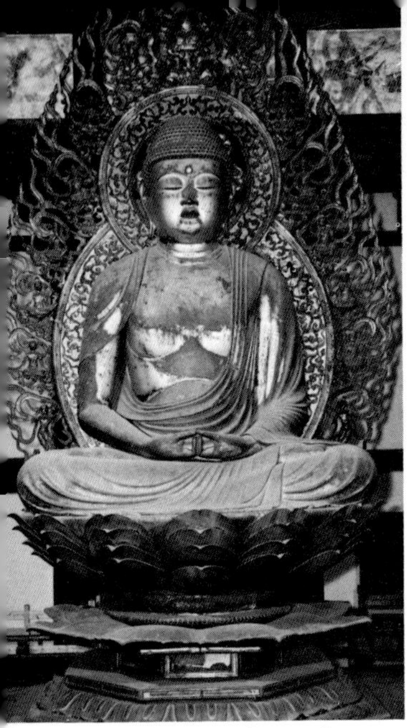

13. Amida Nyorai, seated;
Hokai-ji Temple,
late Heian Period,
Wood, 305 cm

14. Amida Nyorai, seated;
Gokurakubo, Genko-ji Temple
Heian Period, Wood, 156.9 cm

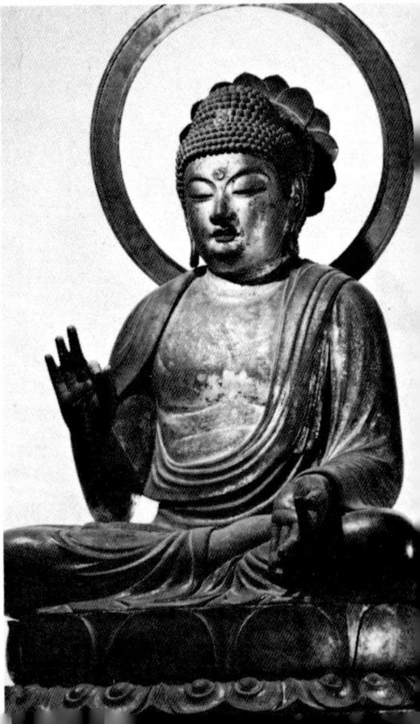

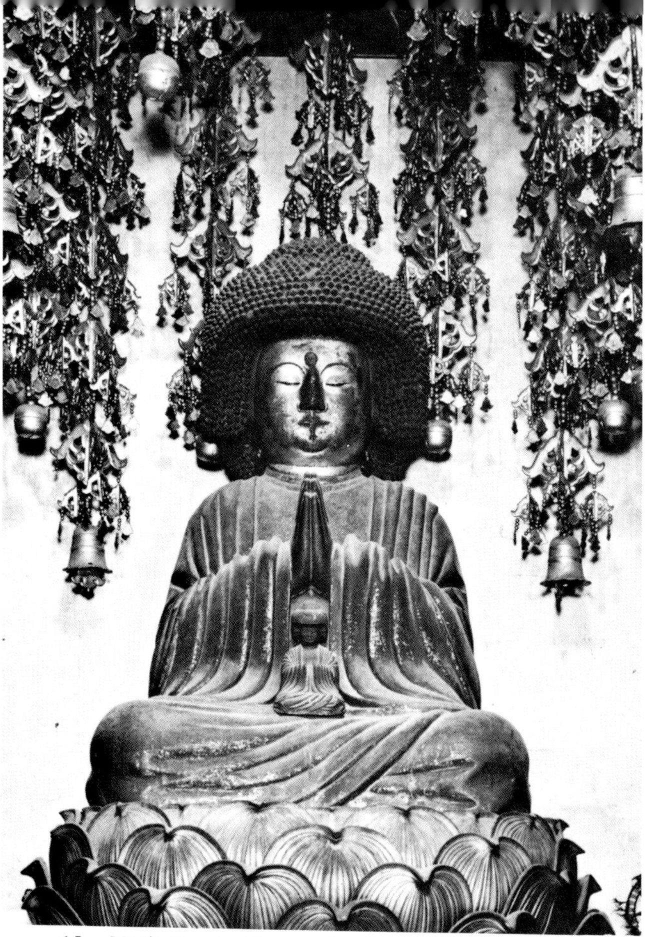

15. Meditating Amida, seated; Kanjinjo (Alms Room), Todai-ji Temple, Kamakura Period, Wood, 106.2 cm

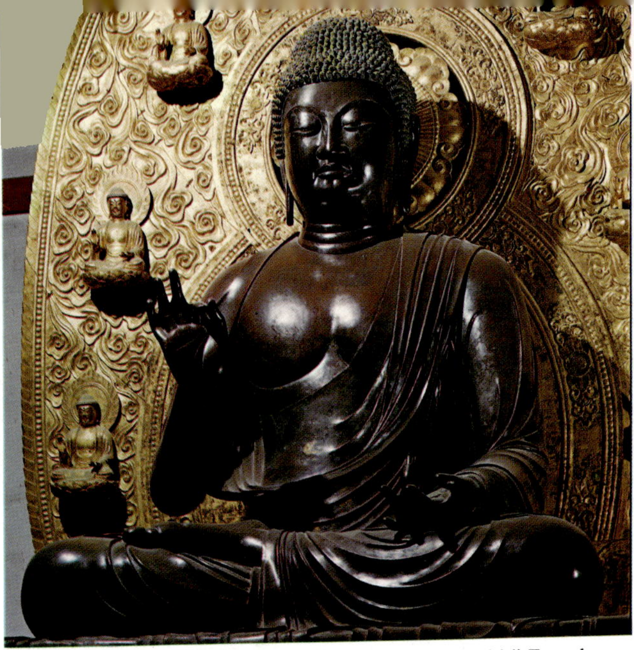

16. **Yakushi Nyorai, seated;** Kondo Hall, Yakushi-ji Temple, early Nara Period, Bronze, 254.7 cm

Yakushi Nyorai has made twelve sacred promises that mainly provide man with material benefits. His seventh promise specifically pledges to relieve man of physical illness and to dispel man's spiritual confusion. It is the best known of Yakushi's twelve sacred promises and has earned him the name "Physician of Souls." Yakushi dwells in the Eastern Pure Land. Buddhist sutras attribute seven mutations to Yakushi. The mutations often appear as tiny images on the main statue's halo.

17. **Yakushi Nyorai, head;** National Treasury Hall, Kofuku-ji Temple, Hakuho Period, Bronze, 97.3 cm

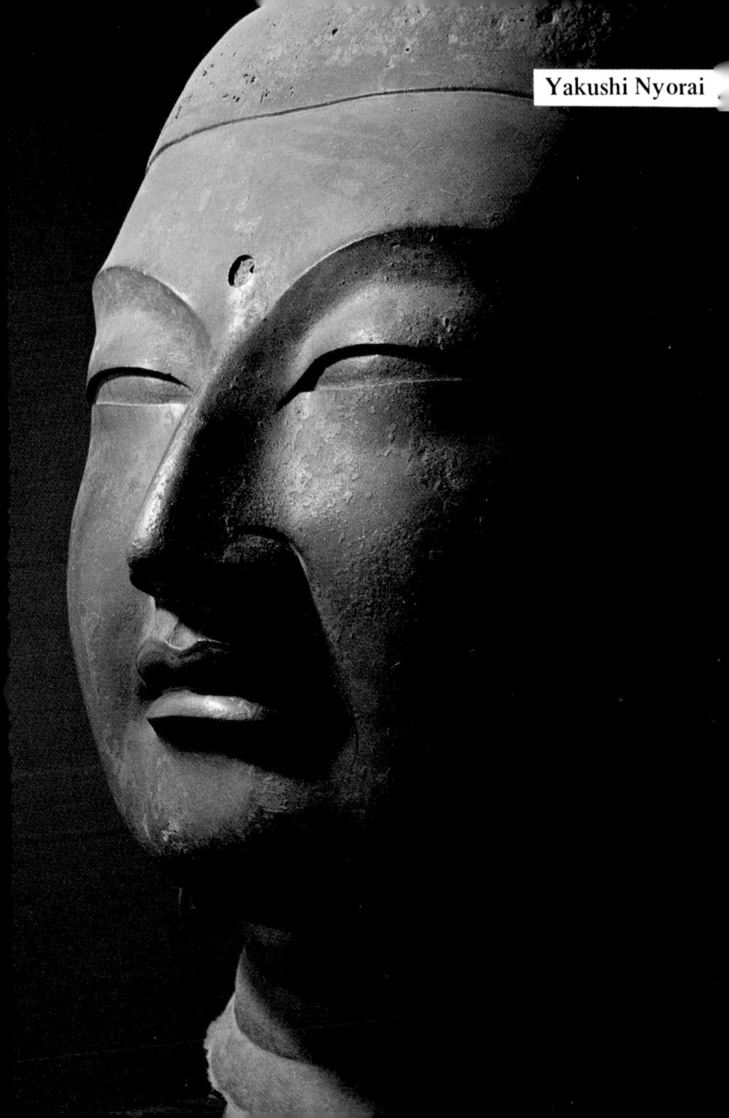

Yakushi Nyorai

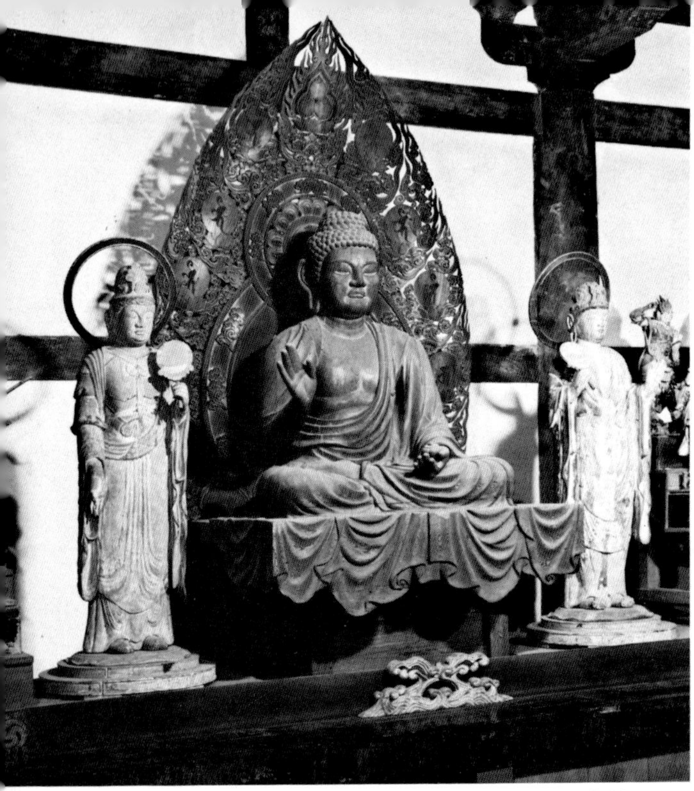

18. Yakushi Nyorai, seated, with attendants Nikko and Gakko; Main Hall, Akishino-dera Temple, Heian Period, Wood, Yakushi 140.5 cm, Nikko 156 cm, Gakko 154.8 cm

19. Yakushi Nyorai, seated; Horin-ji Temple, Asuka Period, ▶ Wood, 105 cm

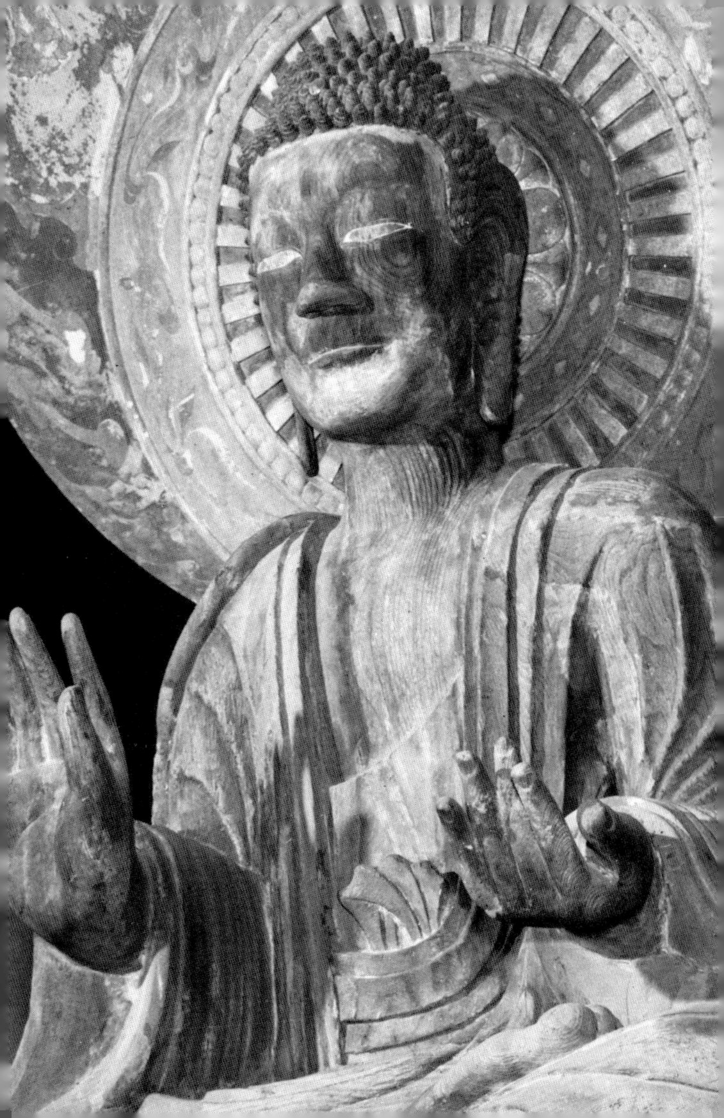

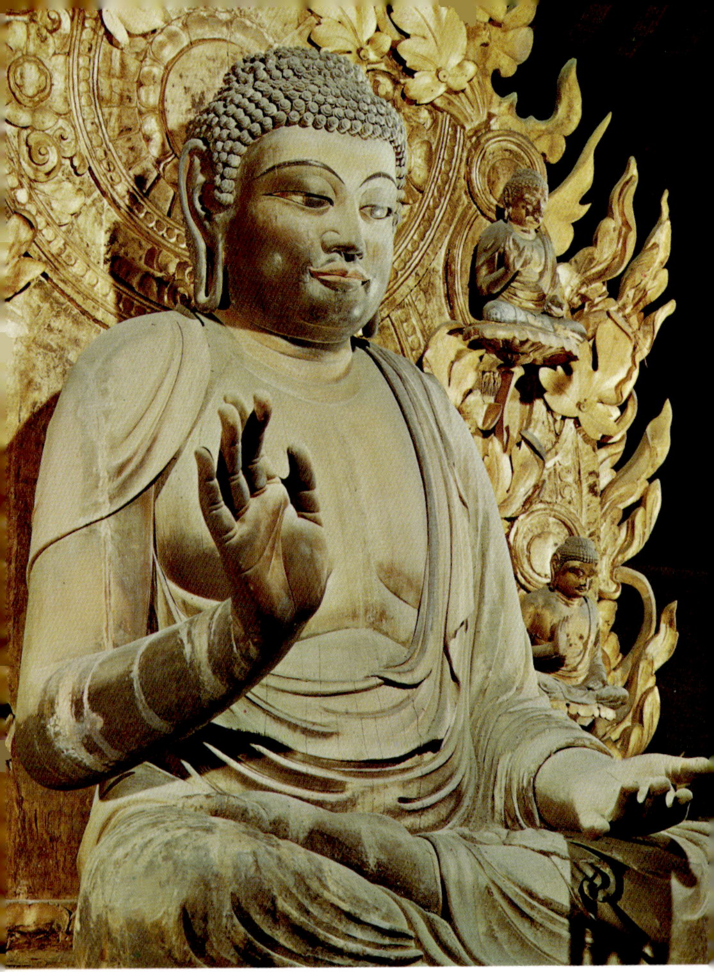

20. Yakushi Nyorai, seated; Main Hall, Shin Yakushi-ji Temple, early Heian Period, Wood, 190.3 cm

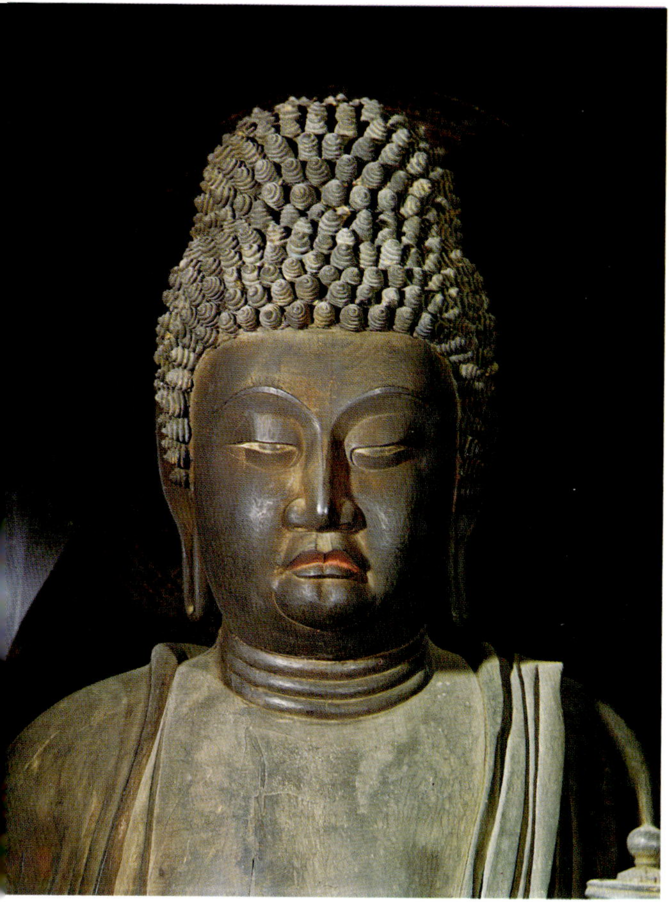

21. Yakushi Nyorai, standing; Jingo-ji Temple, early Heian Period, Wood, 169.6 cm

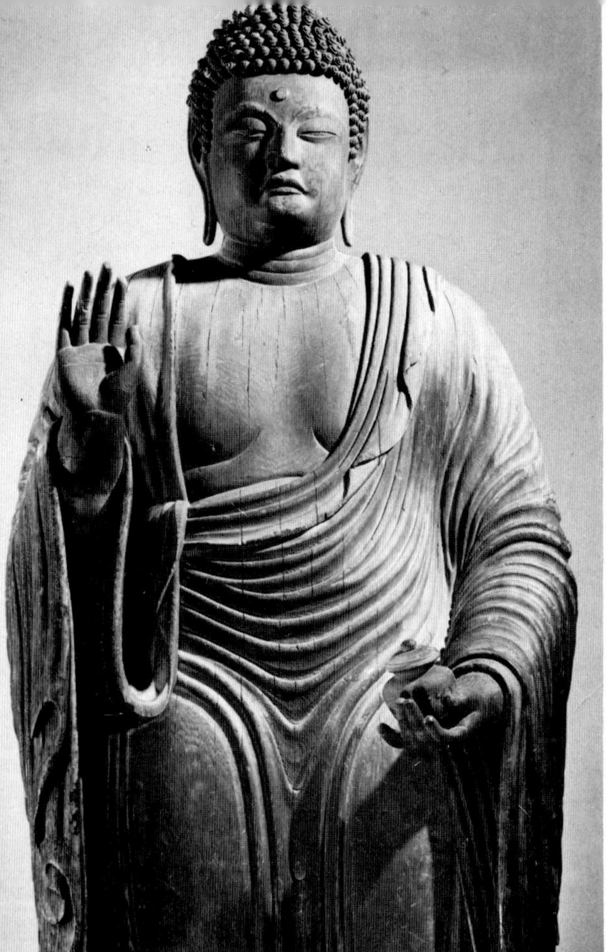

22. Yakushi Nyorai, standing; Genko-ji Temple, early Heian Period, Wood, 165.4 cm

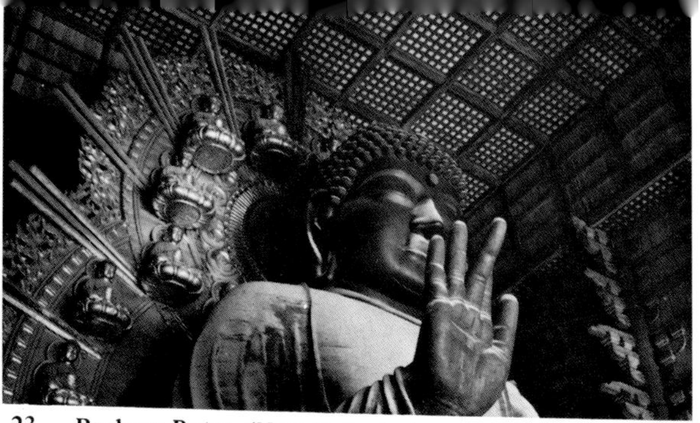

23. Rushana Butsu, (Nara Daibutsu), **seated;** Daibutsu Hall, Todai-ji Temple, Nara Period, Bronze, 14.84 m

Dainichi Nyorai

Todai-ji Temple's Giant Buddha is an image of Rushana Butsu. The first Mahayana sutra describes Buddha sitting on a lotus surrounded by a thousand Shaka, each sitting on a lotus. Each of the thousand lotuses represents ten thousand million nations. Each nation has its own Shaka.

Todai-ji Temple was the central temple of Nara Buddhism, Buddhism which flourished under state sponsorship during the Nara Period (710–794). Emperor Shomu decreed in 741 that two Buddhist temples – one each for priests and nuns – be constructed in every *kuni* in the land. Many of these *Kokubunji* temples – which Todaiji originally was – still stand today. When the giant Rushana Butsu was moved to Nara's Kokubun-ji Temple from Emperor Shomu's Shigaraki Palace, the temple was renamed Todai-ji, the name by which it is known today. Esoteric Buddhism gradually replaced Nara Buddhism beginning in the late eighth century, and in the early ninth century gave the name Dainichi to Rushana Butsu.

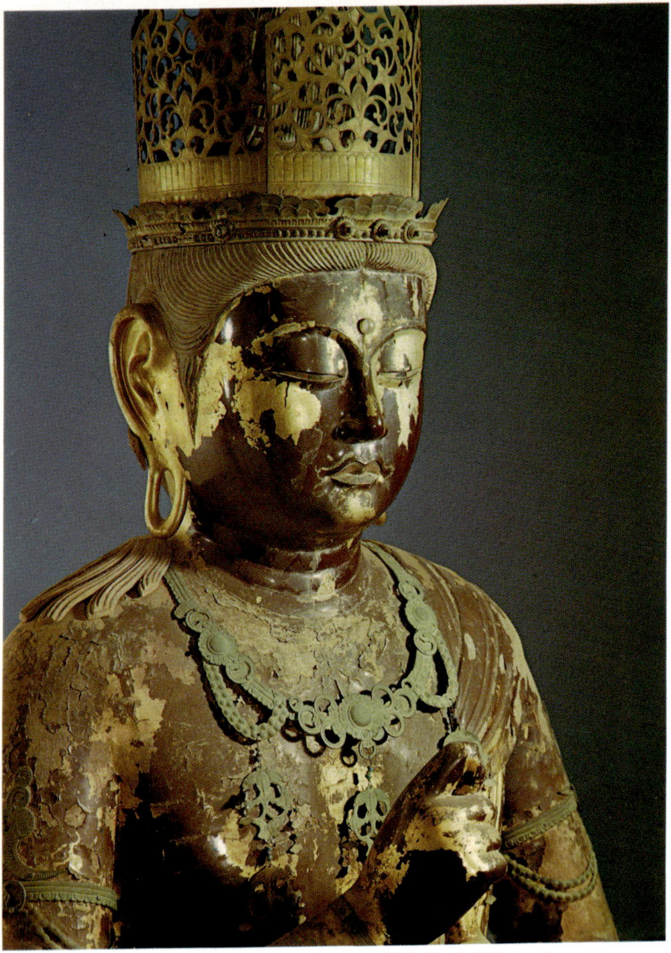

24. Dainichi Nyorai, seated; Main Hall, Enjo-ji Temple, Kamakura Period, Wood, 101 cm

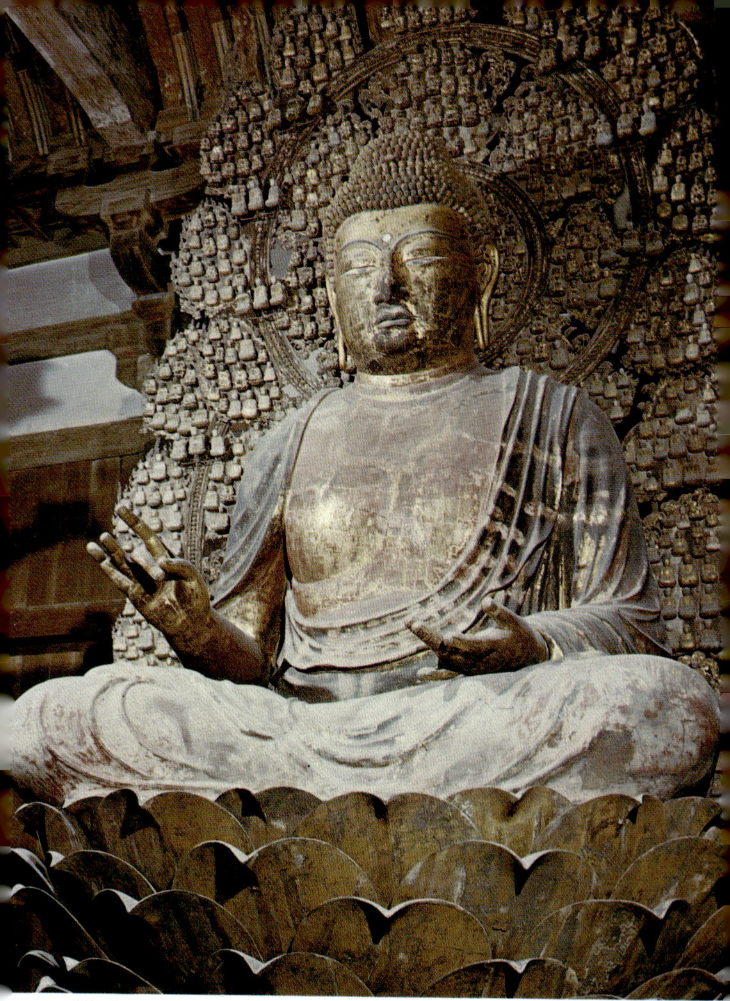

25. Rushana Butsu, seated; Kondo Hall, Toshodai-ji Temple, Nara Period, Dry lacquer, 370 cm

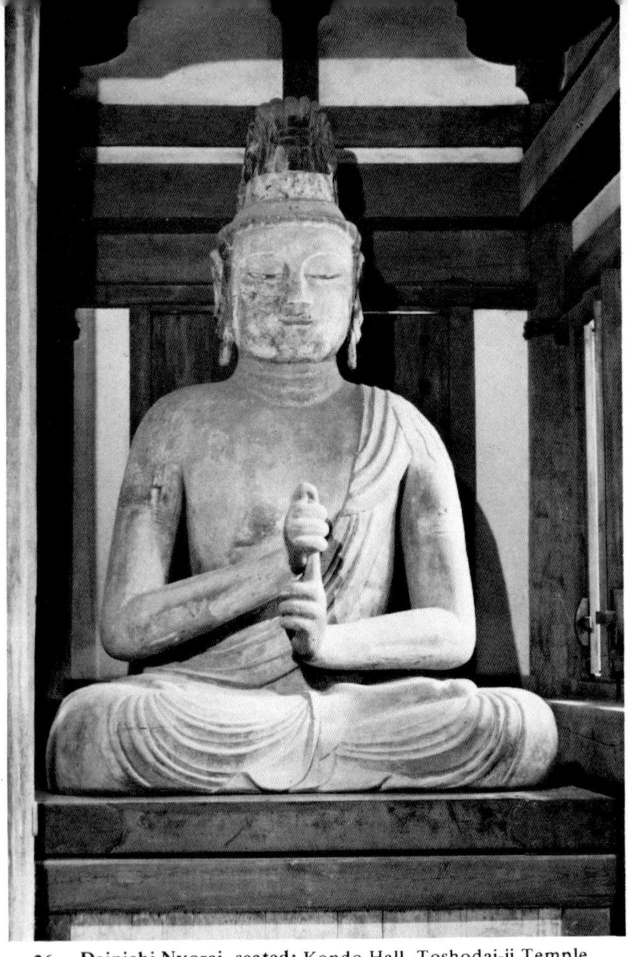

26. **Dainichi Nyorai, seated;** Kondo Hall, Toshodai-ji Temple, early Heian Period, Wood, 330 cm

Miroku Bosatsu

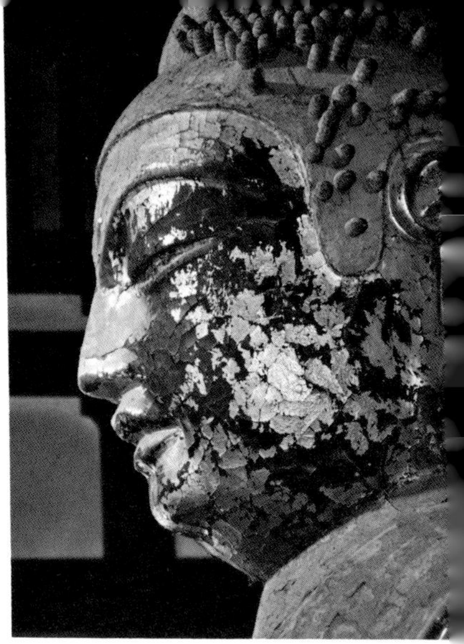

27. Miroku Butsu, seated; Kondo Hall, Taima-dera Temple, Hakuho Period, Stucco, 219 cm

As a name in Sanskrit, Miroku means one born of love or compassion. Miroku was a disciple of Sakyamuni and was promised by the Master that he would one day reach nirvana. He dwells in Tusita, the fourth of six levels of heaven for bodhisattvas, in the Inner Temple of the Palace of Seven Jewels. There he practices austerities, and edifies heavenly beings. Buddhism teaches he will return to earth 56 billion 70 million years after Buddha's death to lead all men down the righteous path, and finally to enter nirvana himself.

Images which depict Miroku in Tusita undergoing austerities or contemplating how best to save mankind are bodhisattva (bosatsu). Miroku Nyorai statues or paintings depict Miroku in nirvana after his second stay on earth.

28. Miroku Bosatsu, half cross-legged; Chugu-ji Temple, Asuka Period, Wood, 132 cm ▶

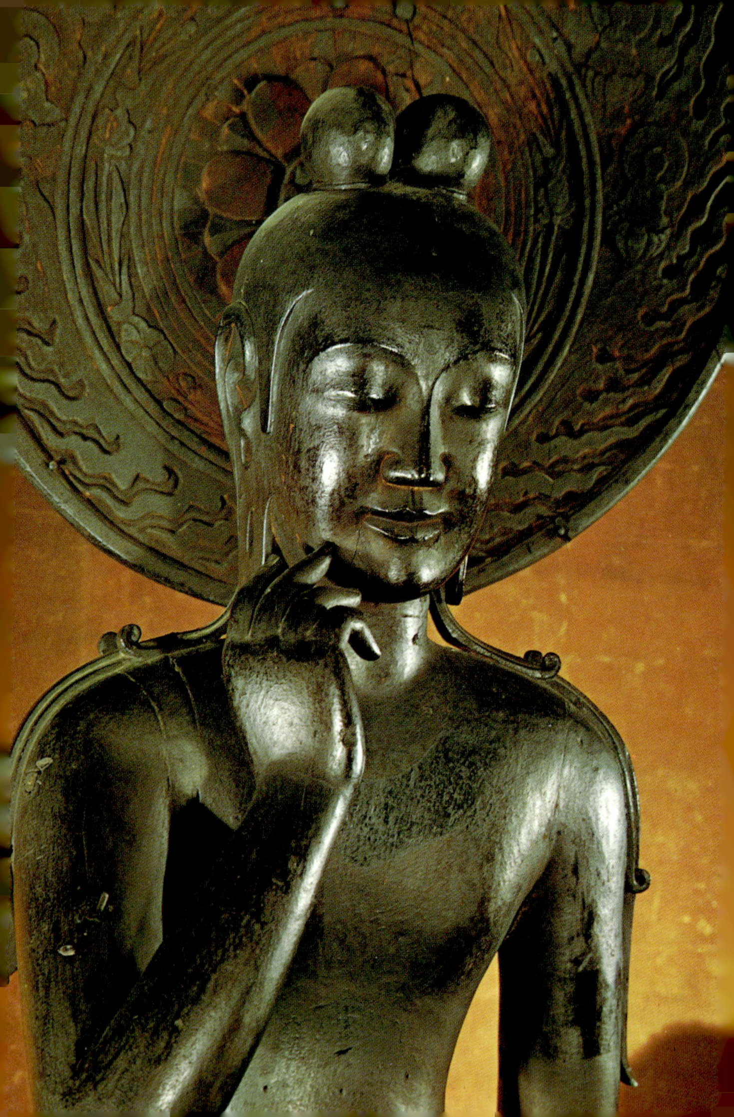

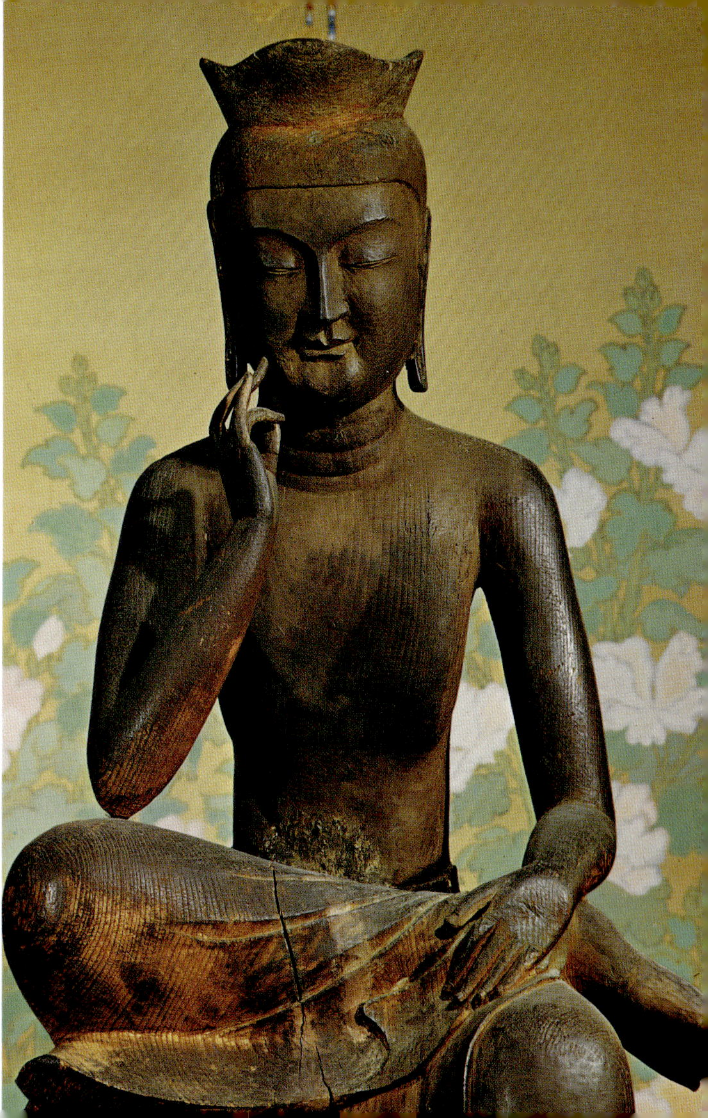

◀ 29. **Miroku Bosatsu, half cross-legged;** Koryu-ji Temple, Asuka Period, Wood, 123.5 cm

30. **Miroku Butsu, seated;** Hokuendo Hall, Kofuku-ji Temple, Kamakura Period, Wood, 142 cm

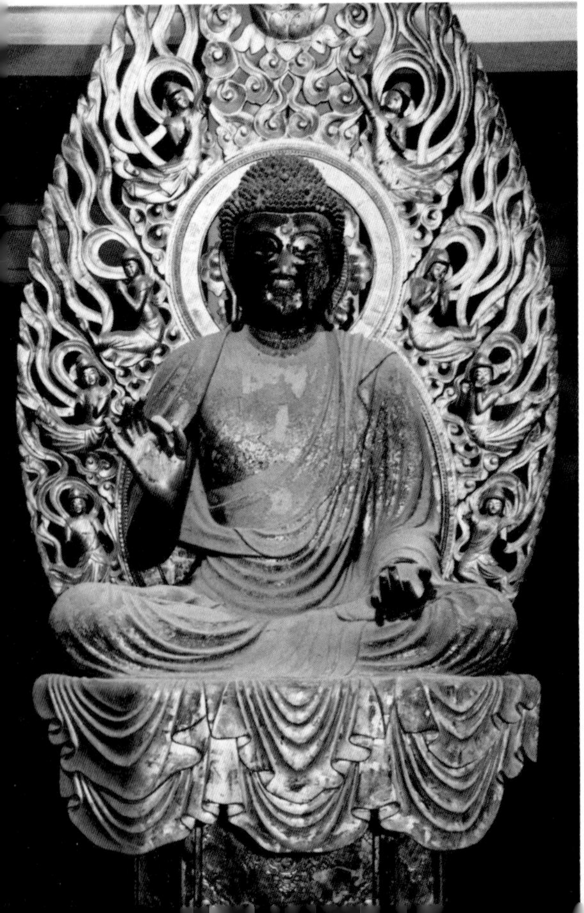

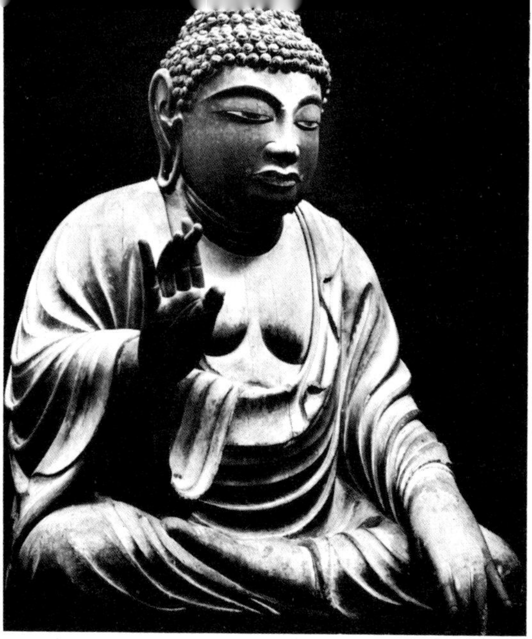

31. Miroku Butsu, seated; Todai-ji Temple, early Heian Period, Wood, 39 cm

Some authorities claim the Mirokubutsu image in Todai-ji Temple is a study completed for the Great Buddha. Two facts contradict this theory. First, the Great Buddha is an image of Rushana Butsu (Dainichi), and the smaller sculpture is clearly Miroku Nyorai. Second, the smaller sculpture dates from the Heian Period (805–1192) while the Rushana Butsu was completed around 743. Although tiny, the Miroku statue expresses great force. That force may have misled those who claim the image is a study for the Great Buddha.

32. Sho Kannon, standing; Toindo Hall, Yakushi-ji Temple, early Nara Period, Bronze, 189 cm ▶

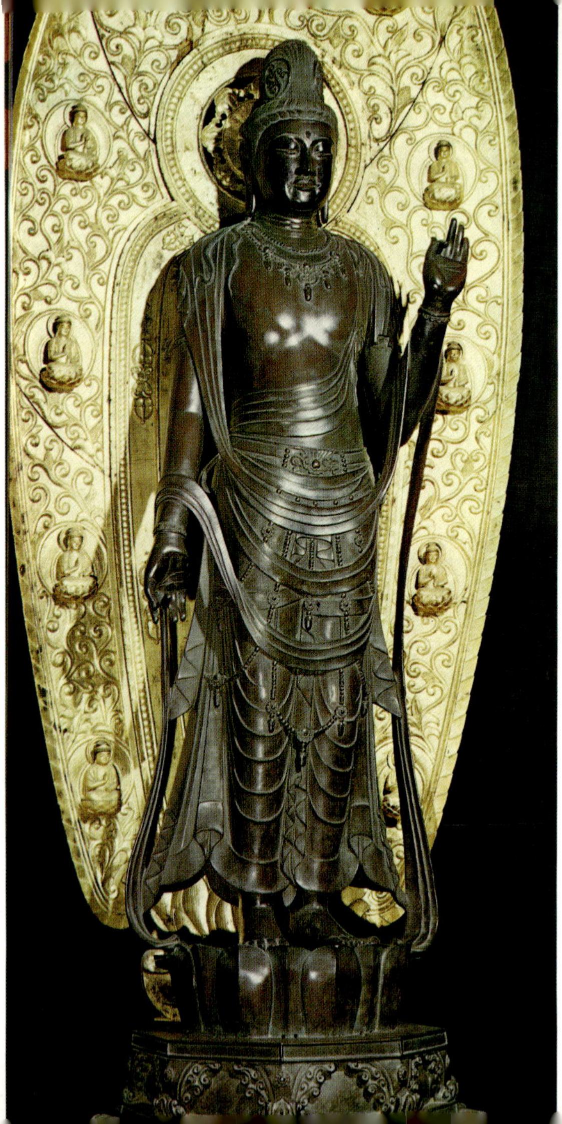

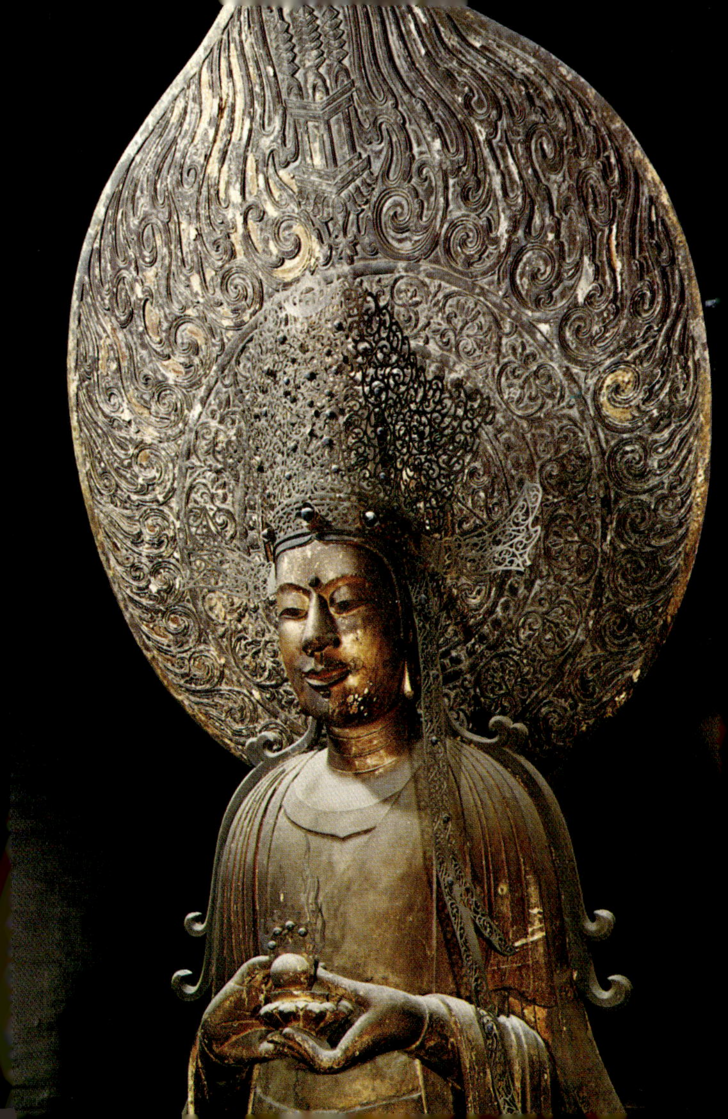

Kannon Bosatsu

Bodhisattvas are individuals filled with loving compassion who rather than enter nirvana after attaining enlightenment choose to remain in the life-death cycle to help redeem other men. Among Japanese the most popular bodhisattvas are Kannon and Jizo. Kannon Bosatsu has been reverred since Buddhism came to Japan, and Kannon images exist that date from the Asuka Period (550–650). The Guze, Kudara, and Yumetagai Kannon images in Horyu-ji Temple not only attract large numbers of worshippers but are notable works of art. Reverence for Kannon spread rapidly after Emperor Hanayama (1249-1305) decreed that thirty-three pilgrimage spots (*sanjusankasho*) be established, one for each of Kannon's thirty-three manifestations. There are sets of *sanjusankasho* in various parts of Japan. The most famous is that of Saigoku (western Japan).

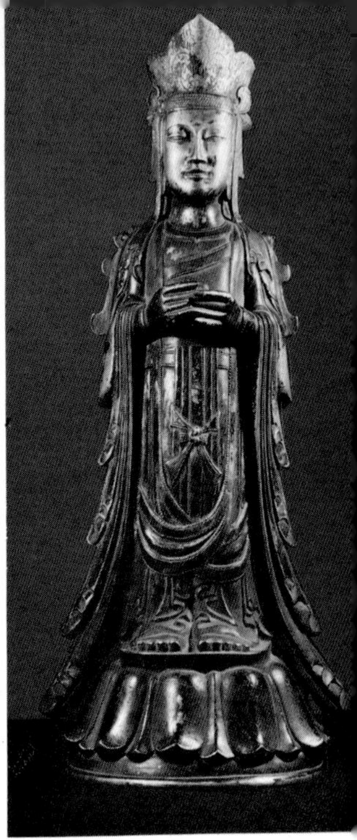

34. Kannon Bosatsu, standing; Hozoden Treasury, Horyu-ji Temple, Asuka Period, Bronz 56.3 cm

◀ 33. **Guze Kannon, Kannon Bosatsu, standing;** Yumedono Hall, Horyu-ji Temple, Asuka Period, Wood, 179.9 cm

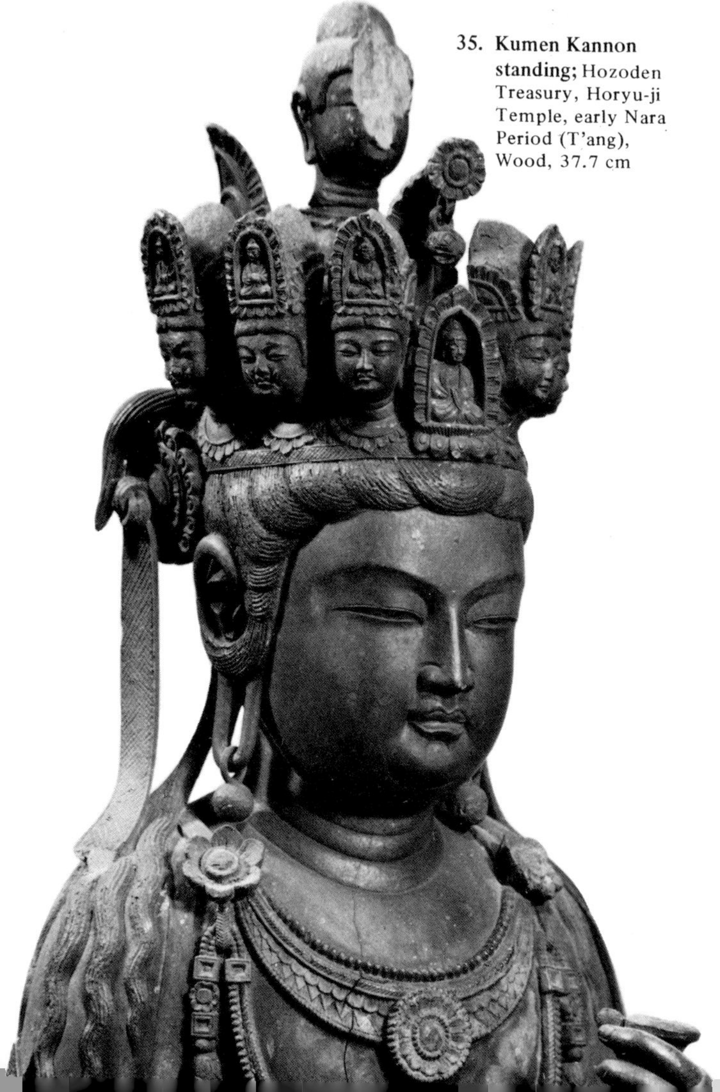

35. Kumen Kannon standing; Hozoden Treasury, Horyu-ji Temple, early Nara Period (T'ang), Wood, 37.7 cm

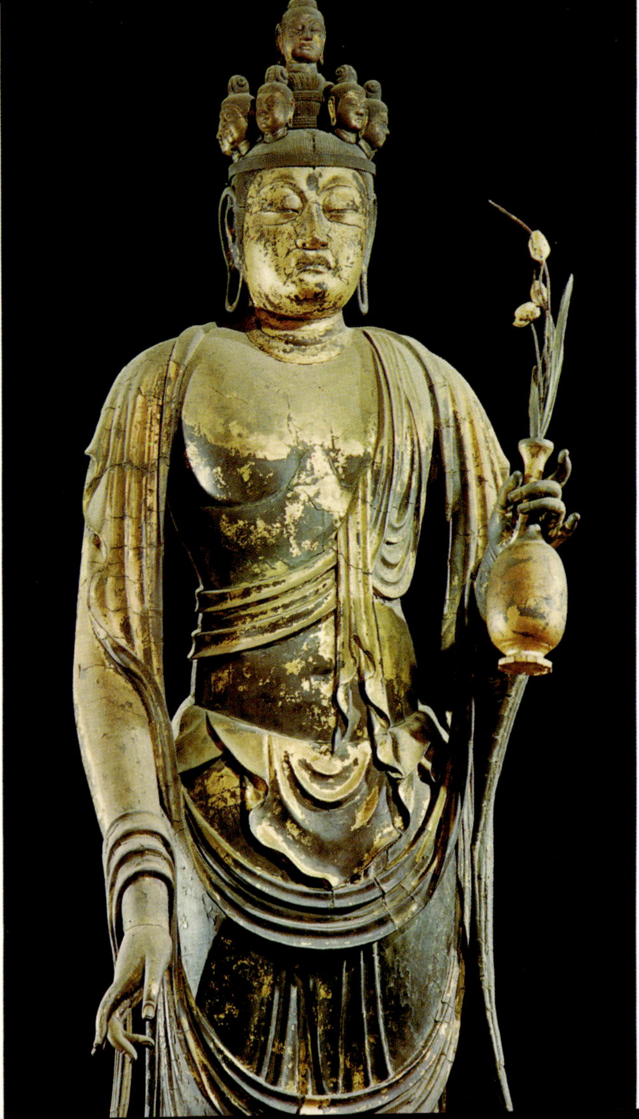

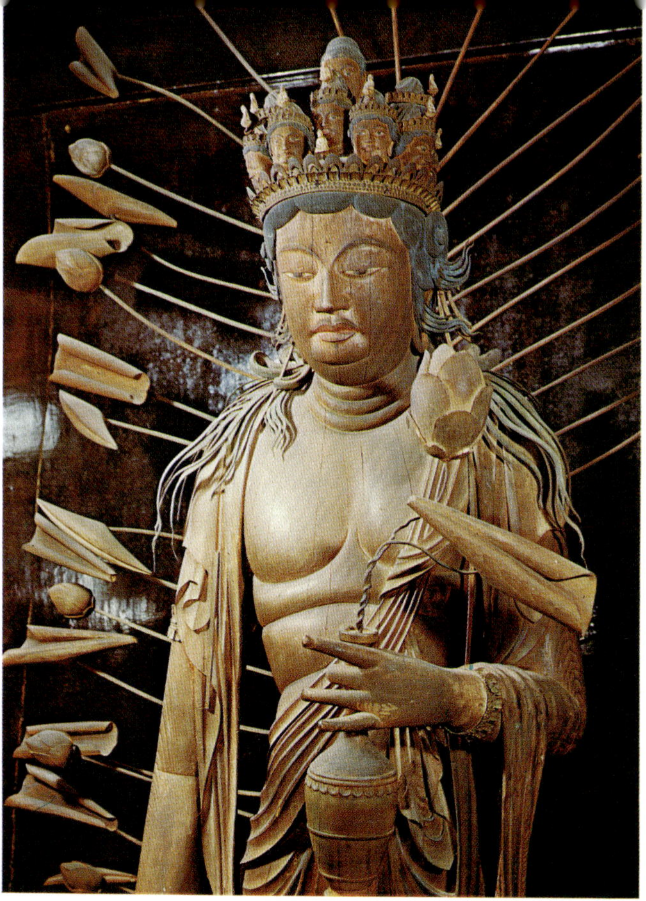

37. **Juichimen Kannon, standing;** Main Hall, Hokke-ji Temple, early Heian Period, Wood, 100 cm

◀ 36. **Juichimen Kannon, standing;** Main Hall, Shorin-ji Temple, Nara Period, Dry lacquer, 227.7 cm

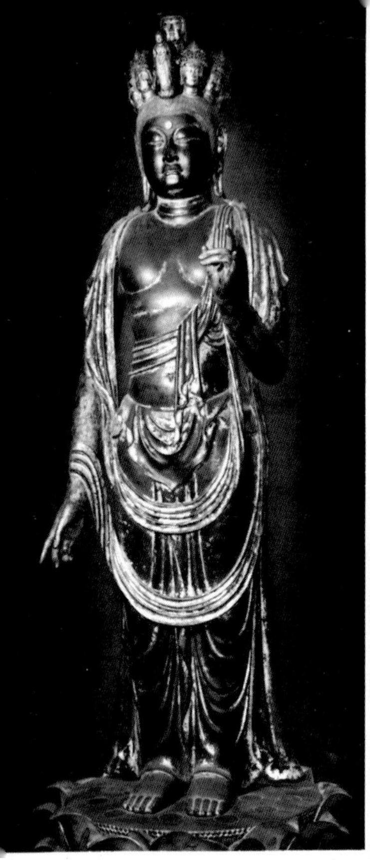

38. **Juichimen Kannon, standing;**
Kannon-ji Temple, Nara Period,
Dry lacquer, 172.2 cm

39. **Juichimen Kannon standing;**
▼ Kondo Hall, Muro-ji Temple,
early Heian Period,
Wood, 212.5 cm

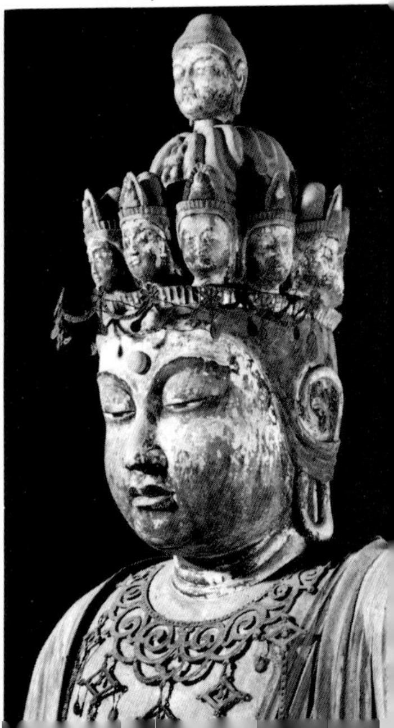

Kannon Bosatsu has thirty-three manifestations. He chooses a particular manifestation to fit the individual soul imploring his help. The Japanese people has reverred the Juichimen (eleven countenances) Kannon since the Nara Period. Among the eleven countenances are those that express benevolence, compassion, and wrath. There is also a smiling countenance, and one that bares canine teeth. Each expression attracts interest for its distinct characteristics.

40. Juichimen Kannon, standing; Domyo-ji Temple, early Heian Period, Wood, 97.9 cm

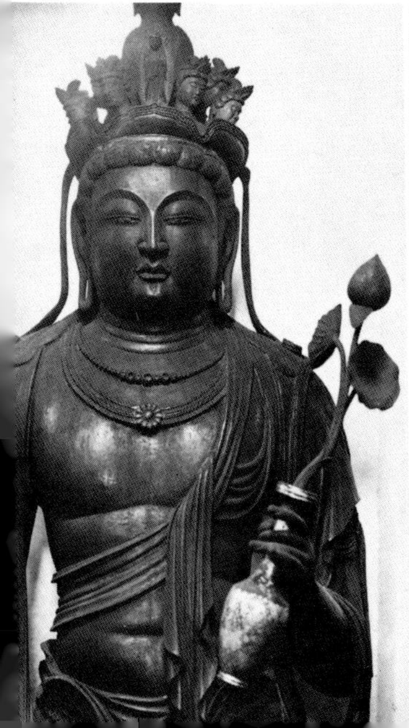

41. Juichimen Kannon, standing; Horin-ji Temple, early Heian Period, Wood, 357.5 cm

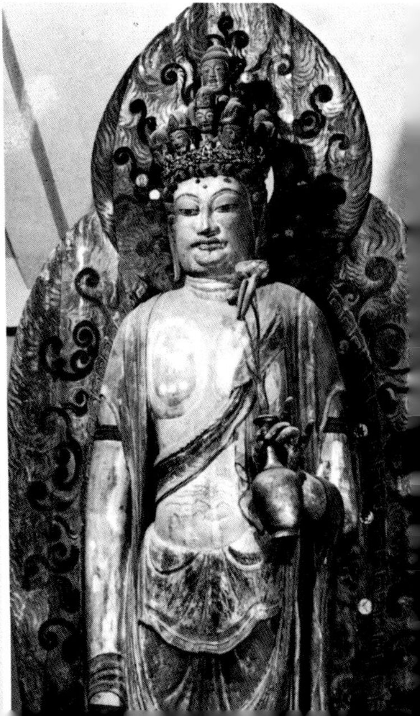

To aid those souls who do not respond to either love or wrath, Kannon comes equipped with a fish line and a strong rope for holding beasts in leash. Among the masses there certainly are men who refuse salvation and act like wild beasts or like fish floundering in the sea.

42. Fuku Kenjaku Kannon, standing; Sangatsudo Hall, Todai-ji Temple, Nara Period, Dry Lacquer, 394 cm

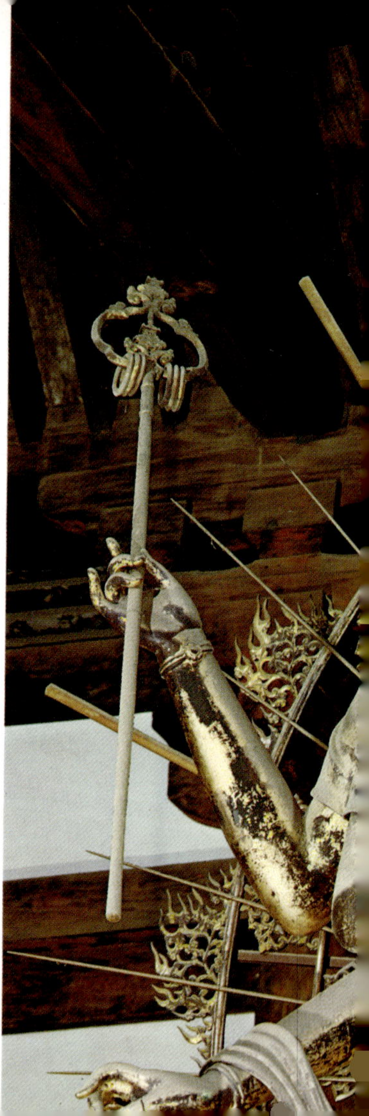

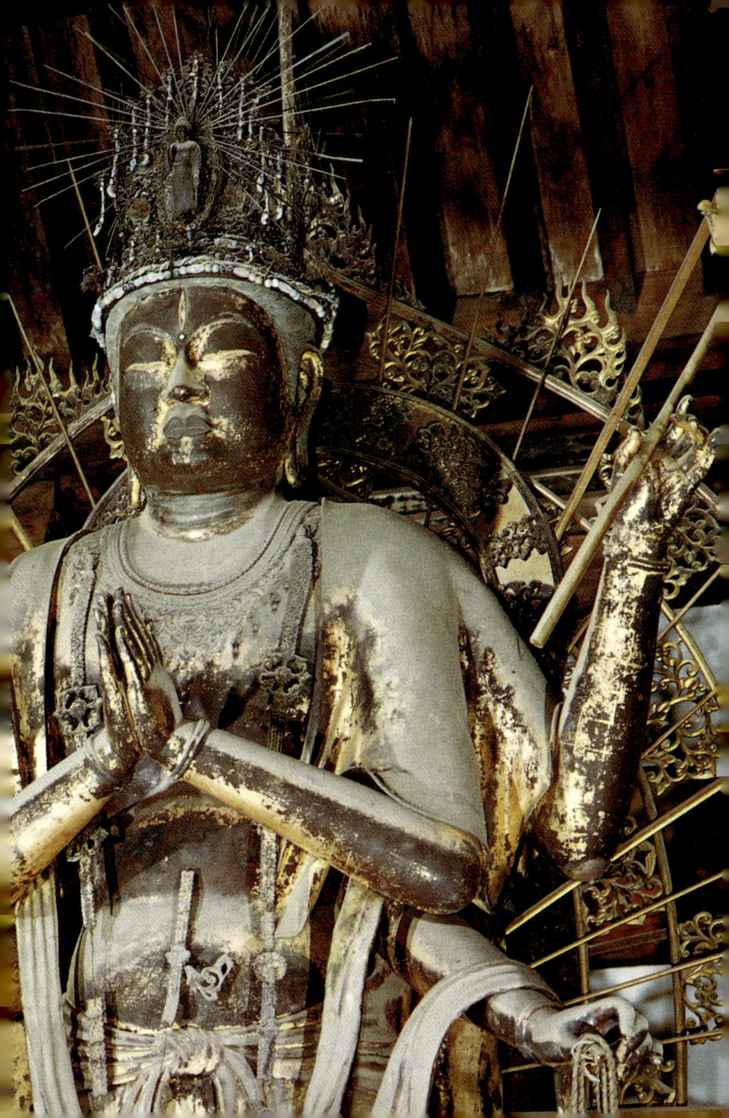

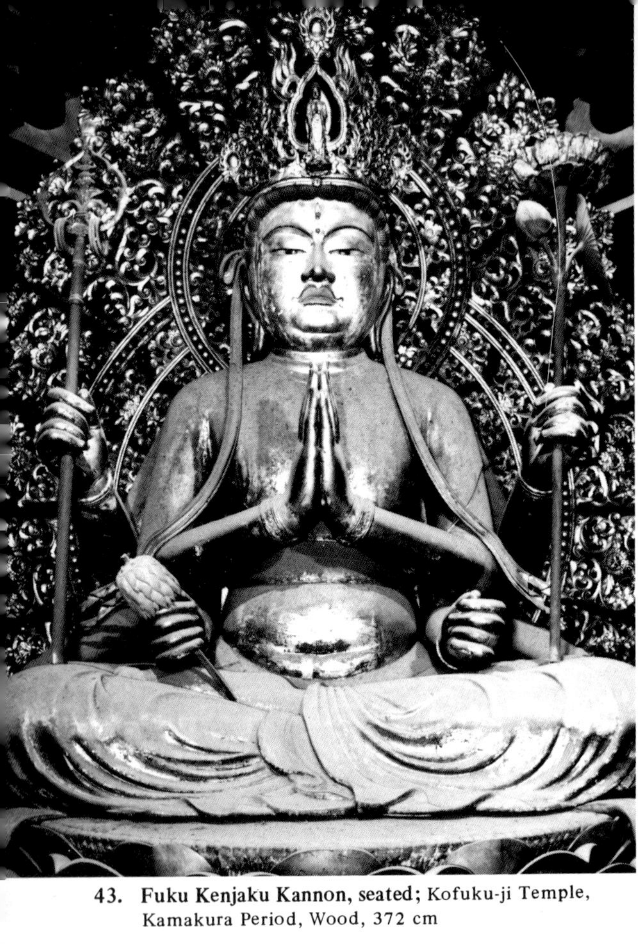

43. **Fuku Kenjaku Kannon, seated;** Kofuku-ji Temple, Kamakura Period, Wood, 372 cm

44. **Fuku Kenjaku Kannon, standing;** ▶ Daian-ji Temple, Nara Period, Wood, 193 cm

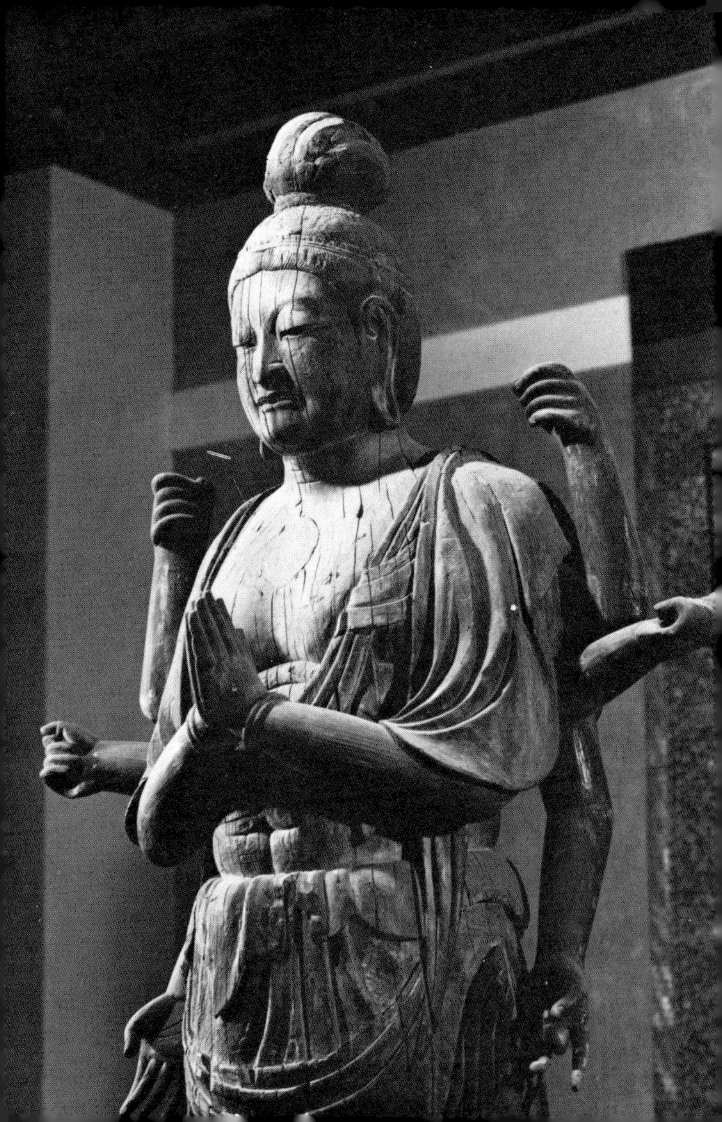

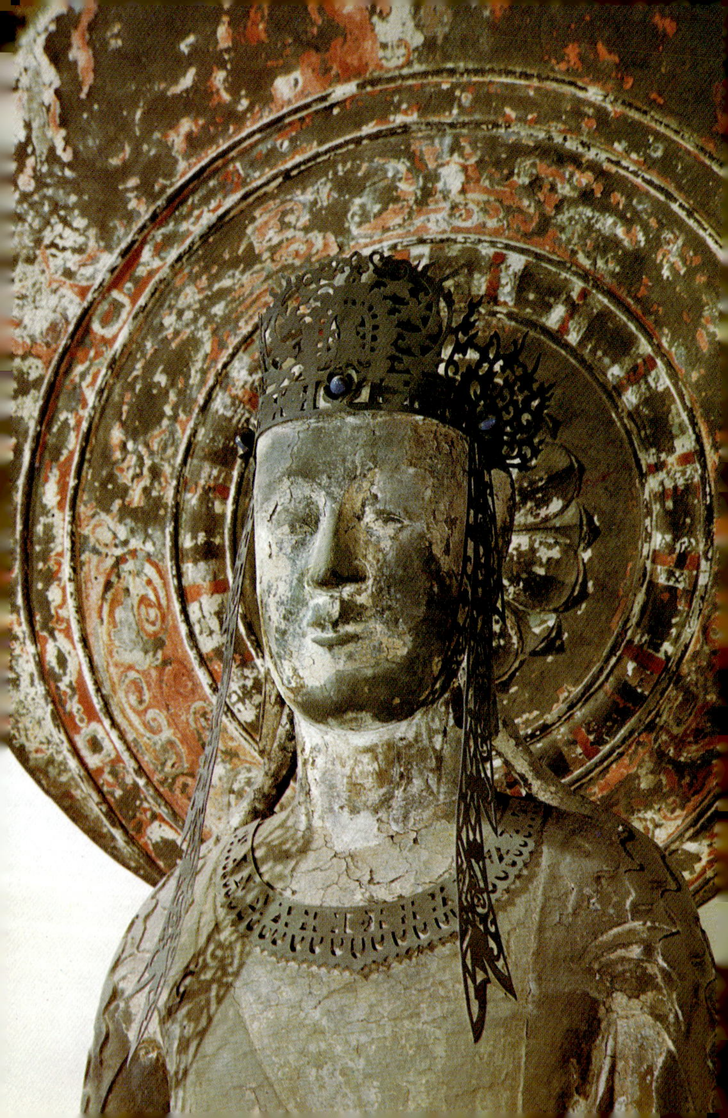

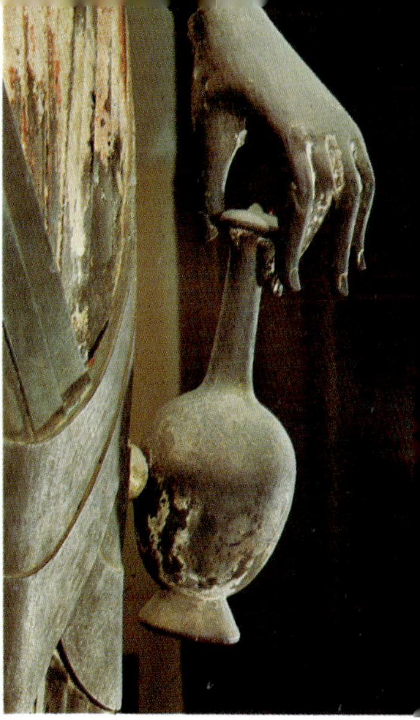

46. **Kudara (Paekche) Kannon,**
detail, same as 45

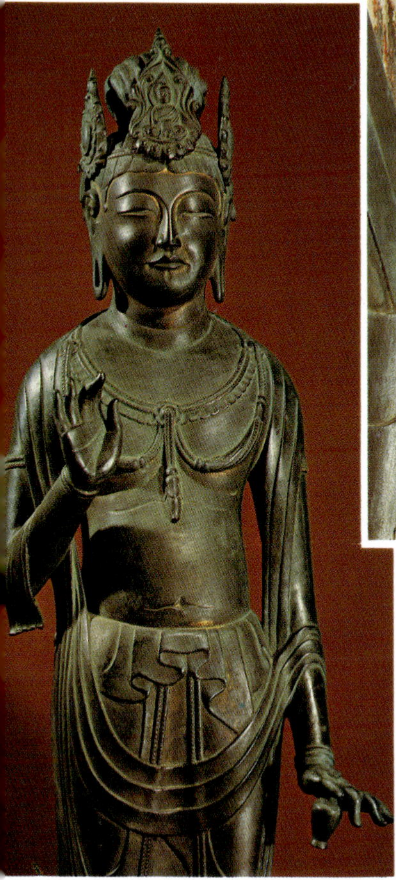

47. **Yumetagae Kannon, standing;**
Hozoden Treasury, Horyu-ji Temple
Hakuho Period, Bronze, 87.9 cm

45. **Kudara (Paekche) Kannon, standing;** Hozoden Treasury,
Horyu-ji Temple, Asuka Period, Wood, 209.4 cm

Bodhisattva Nyoirin Kannon promises salvation to those who will take to their hearts the words of Buddha. He has long been reverenced as personifying a wondrous jewel which purifies contaminated water, vanquishes all evils, and moves the most stoic of men. The wondrous jewel can also bestow great material riches.

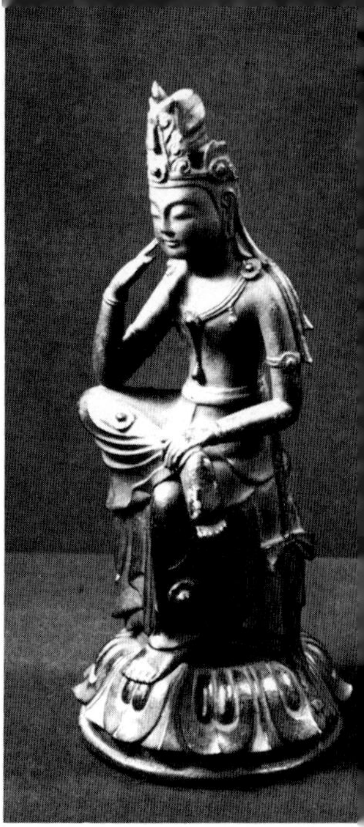

48. **Nyoirin Kannon, half cross-legged;** Oka-dera Temple, Nara Period, Bronze, 31.5 cm

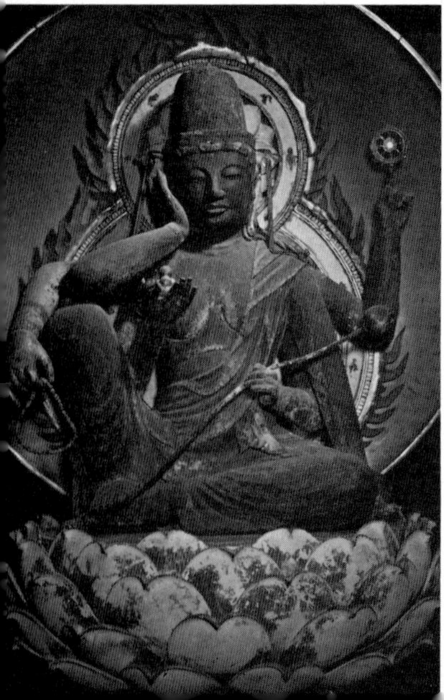

49. **Nyoirin Kannon, seated;** Muro-ji Temple, early Heian Period, Wood, 78.8 cm

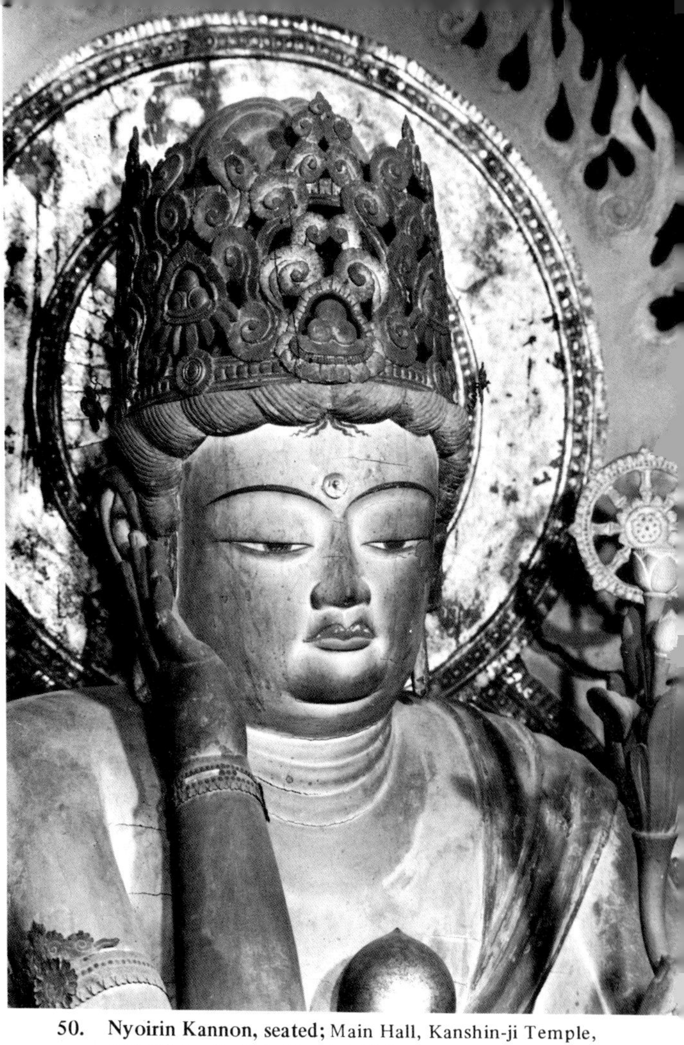

50. Nyoirin Kannon, seated; Main Hall, Kanshin-ji Temple, early Heian Period, Wood, 108.8 cm

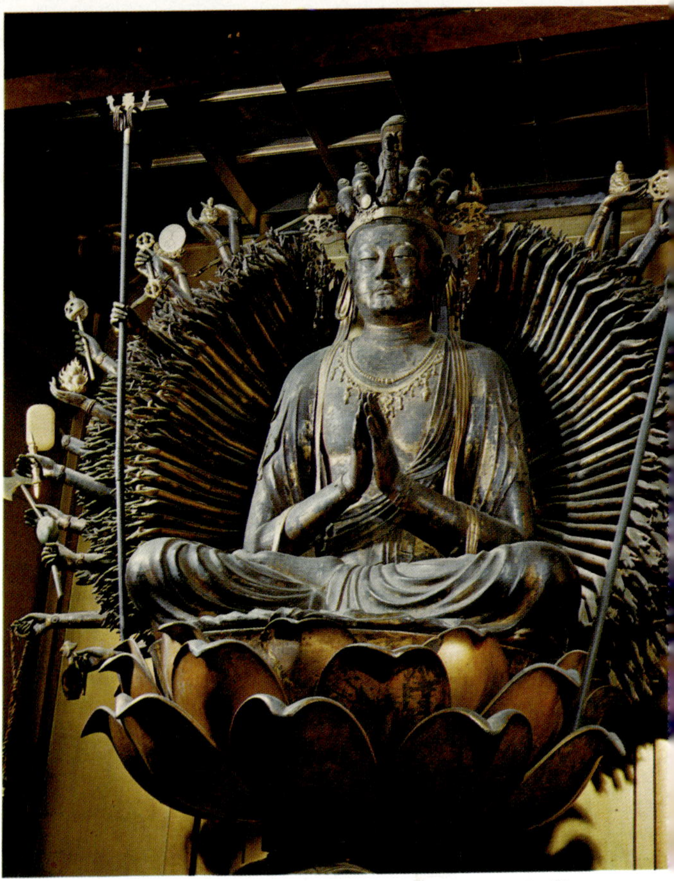

51. Senju Kannon, seated; Main Hall, Fujii-dera Temple, Nara Period, Dry lacquer, 145 cm

52. Senju Kannon, standing; Kondo Hall, Toshodai-ji Temple Nara Period, Dry lacquer, 550 cm

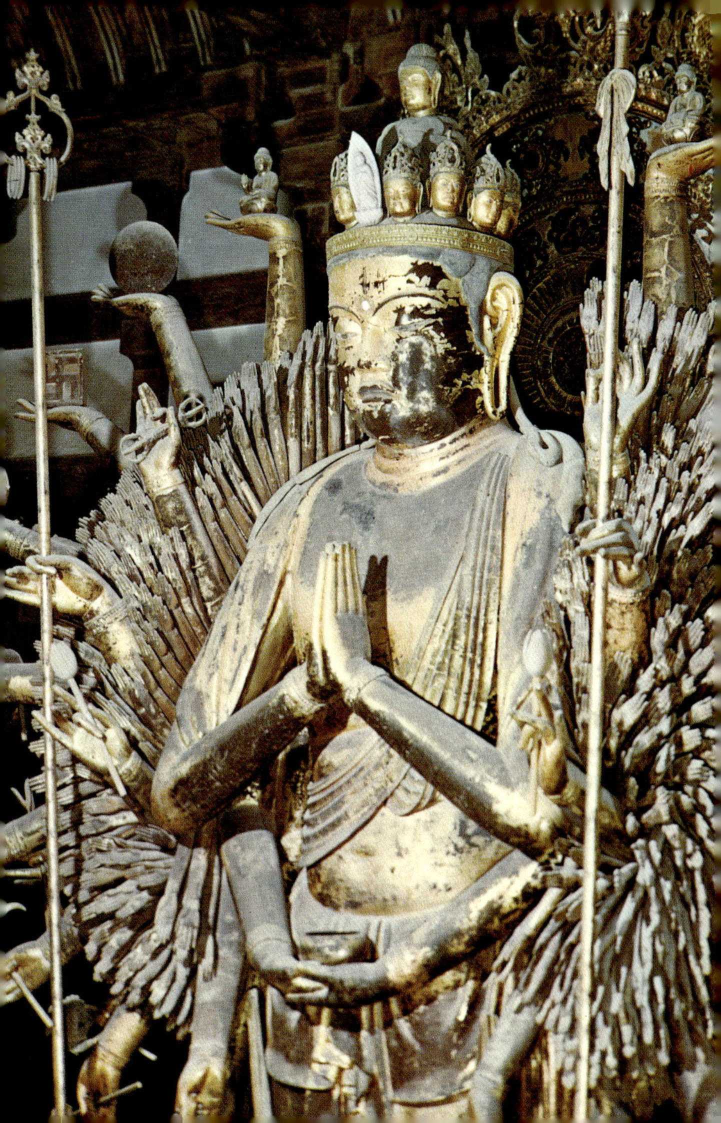

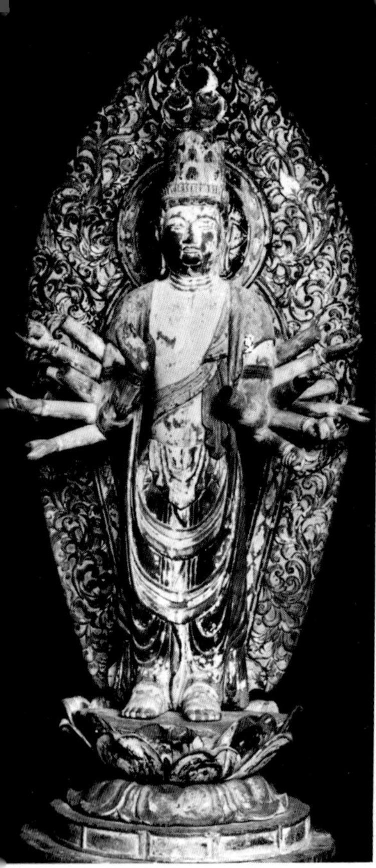

53. **Juntei Kannon, standing;** Shin Yakushi-ji Temple, late Heian Period, Wood, 111.2 cm

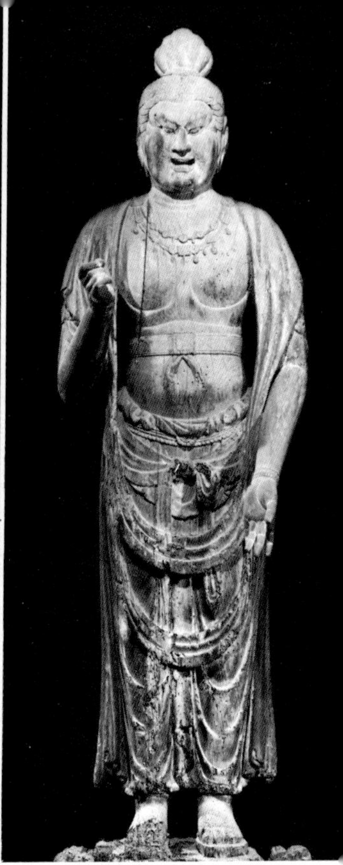

54. **Yoryu Kannon, standing;** Daian-ji Temple, Nara Period, Wood, 171.5 cm

Man beseeches forgiveness for his sins even as he asks for multitudinous material comforts and benefits. To receive the flow of complex and numerous human requests, Kannon is manifested in various ways. Juntei Kannon purifies everything he touches and has the power and influence to grant most of man's wishes. On occasion, a thousand-handed, thousand-headed Kannon is required to save man. Bato Kannon is dreadfully wrathful in appearance and forces or frightens man to tread the path of righteousness.

55. Bato Kannon, standing; Daian-ji Temple, Nara Period, Wood, 159 cm

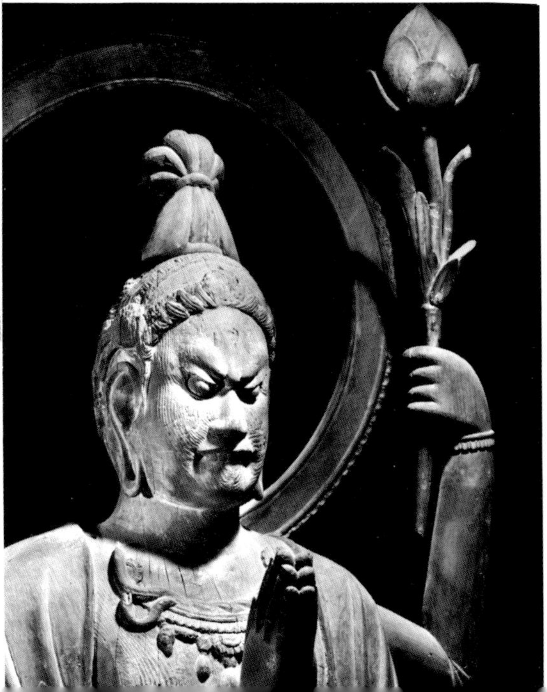

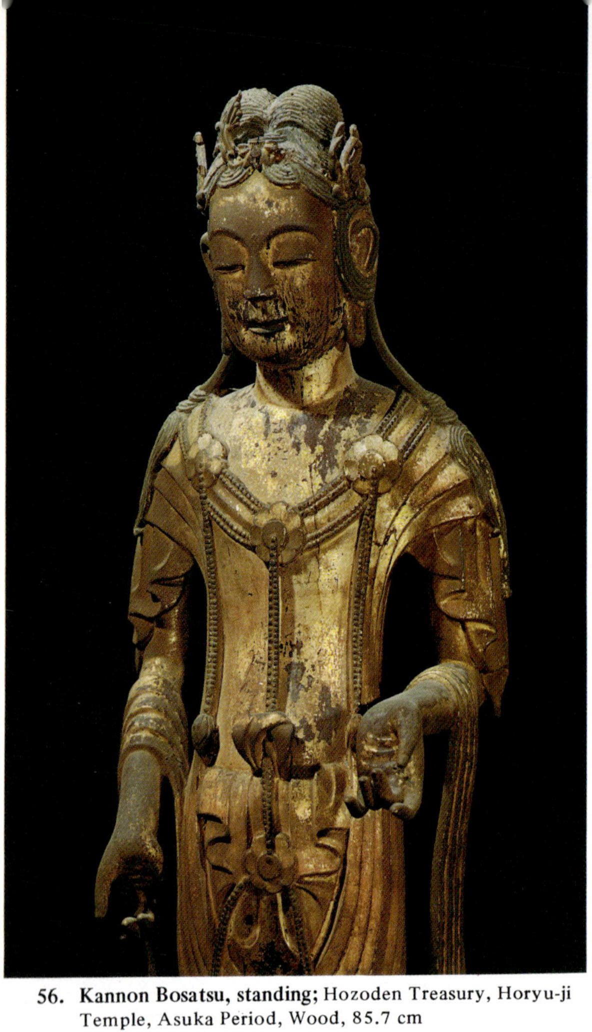

56. Kannon Bosatsu, standing; Hozoden Treasury, Horyu-ji Temple, Asuka Period, Wood, 85.7 cm

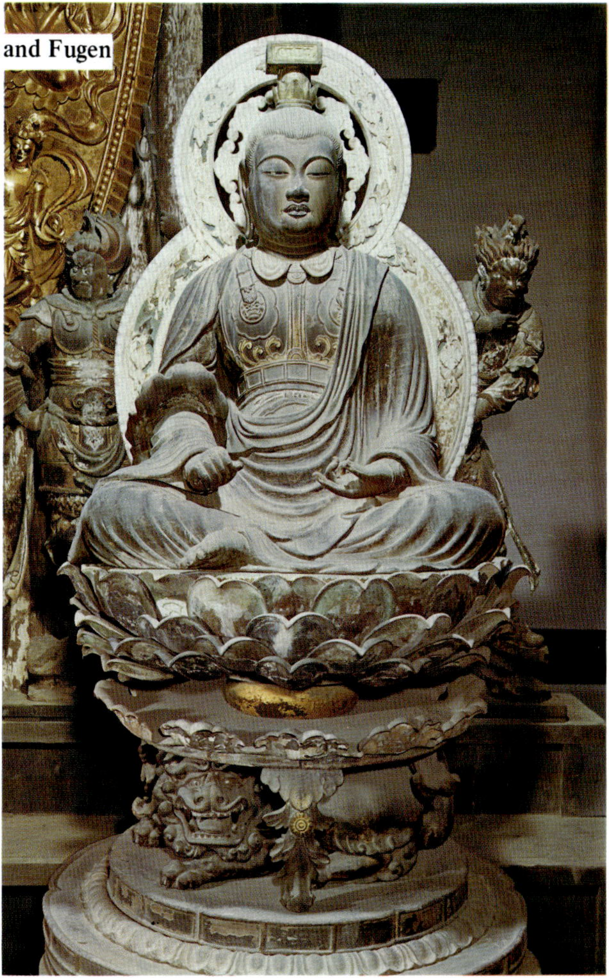

57. Monju Bosatsu, seated; Higashi Kondo Hall, Kofuku-ji Temple, Kamakura Period, Wood, 97 cm

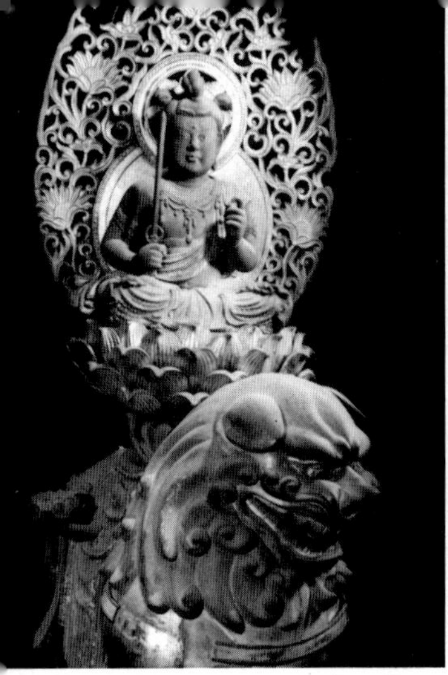

58. Monju Bosatsu, seated on lion; Hannya-ji Temple, Kamakura Period, Wood, over-all 140.6 cm, image 47 cm

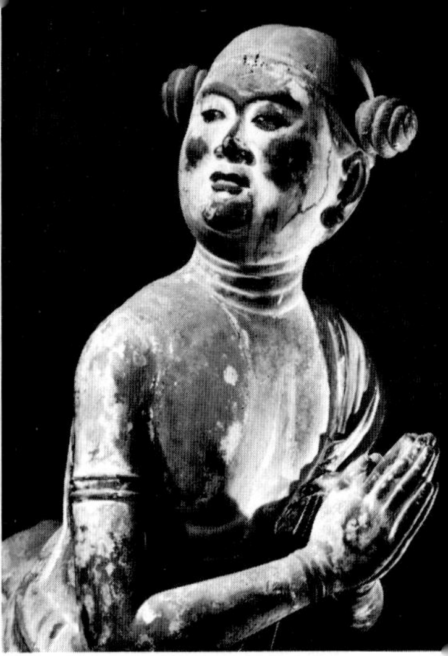

59. Zenzai Doji; Monju-in Temple, Kamakura Period, Wood, 134.5 cm

Images of the bodhisattvas Monju and Fugen will occasionally be found independently but usually appear attending Shaka Nyorai. Monju frequently rides a lion, and Fugen an elephant. They are both popular bodhisattva with many followers. Monju presages happy events and administers the distribution of wisdom. Wisdom refers not merely to the brain's intelligence but includes common sense, and ingeniousness and resourcefulness in everyday living. A Monju image commonly occupies a prominent position in a temple's dining area. Monju's hair is either tied into one, five, or eight knots, or his head is shaven clean like a monk's. Zenzai Doji and other attendants accompany Fugen in crossing the sea.

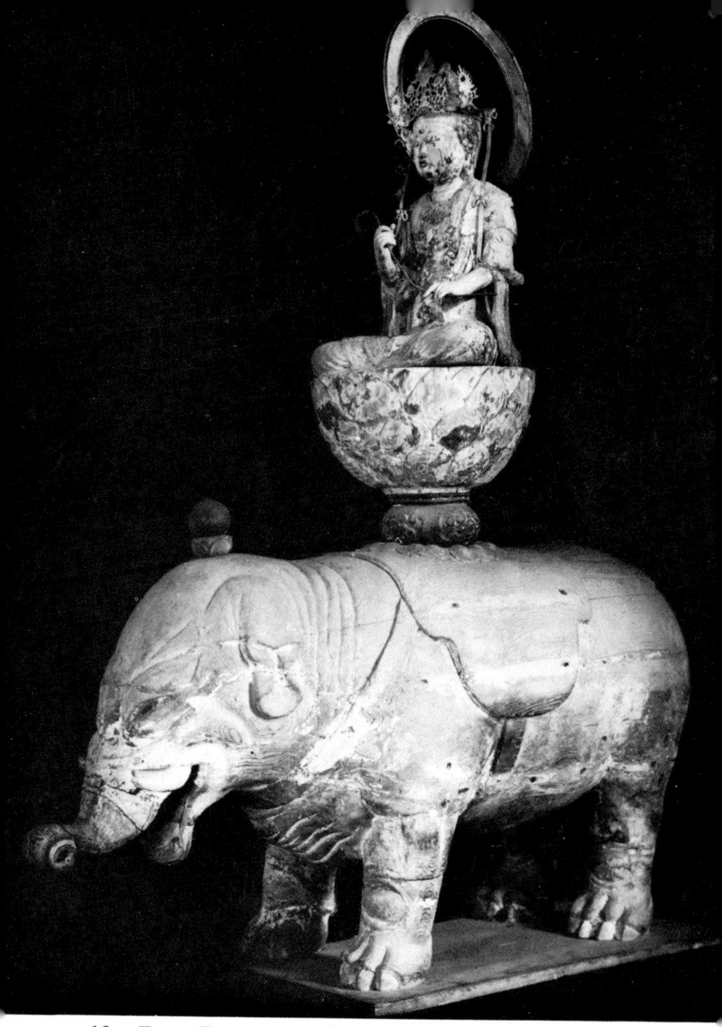

60. Fugen Bosatsu, seated on elephant; Shigatsudo Hall, Todai-ji Temple, Muromachi Period, Wood, 150 cm

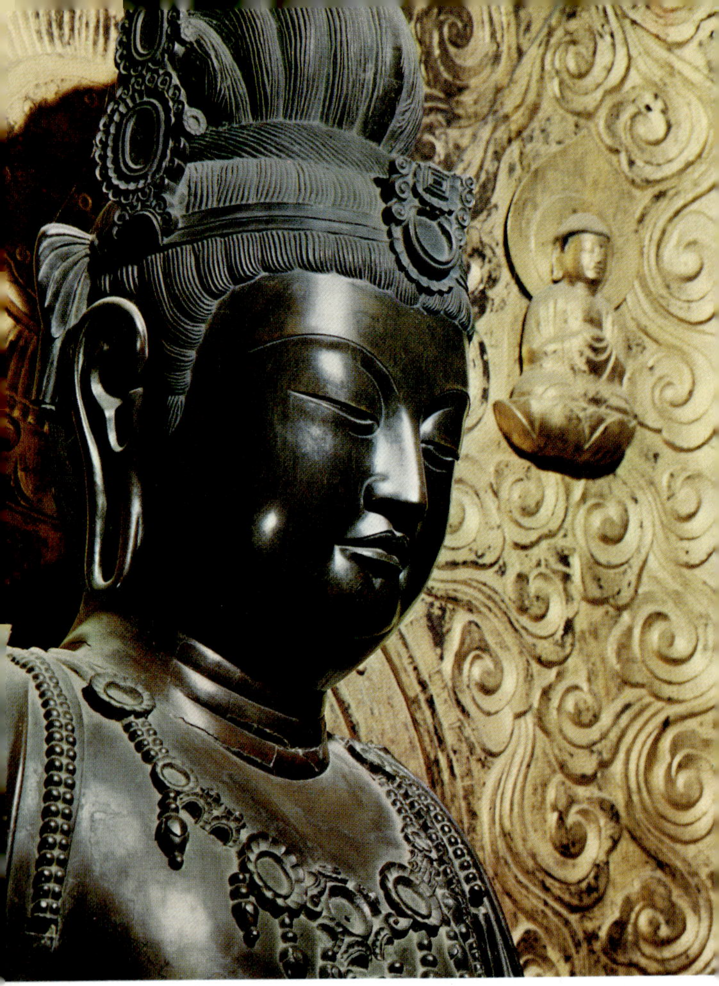

62. **Gakko Bosatsu**, detail, same as 61

61. **Gakko Bosatsu, standing;** Kondo Hall, Yakushi-ji Temple, early Nara Period, Bronze, 315.3 cm

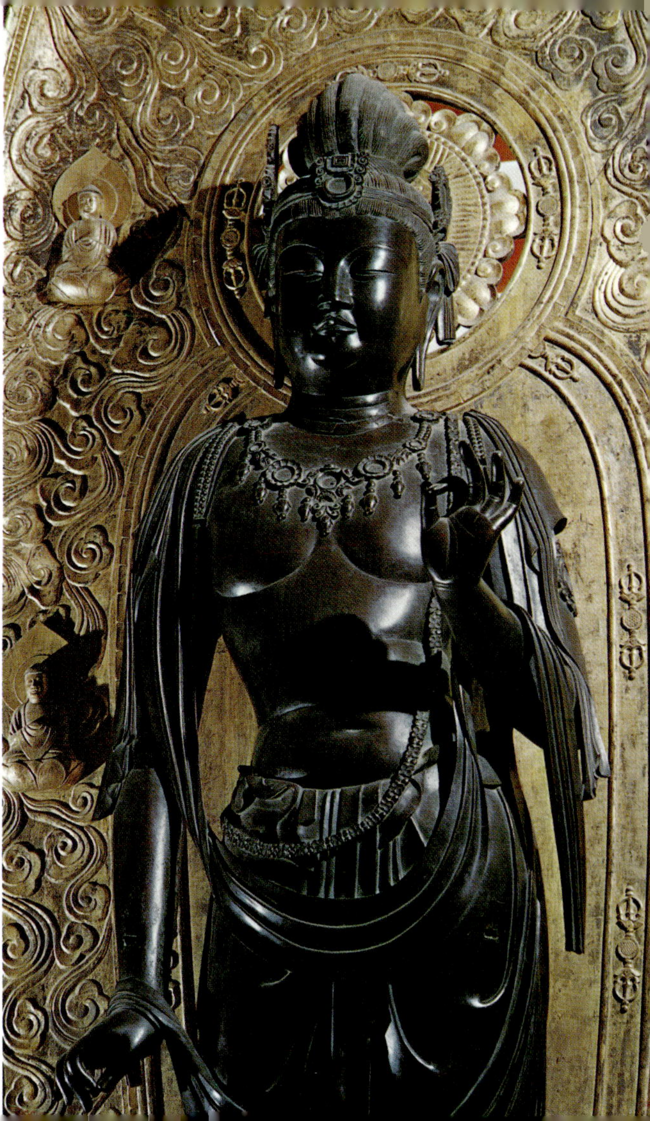

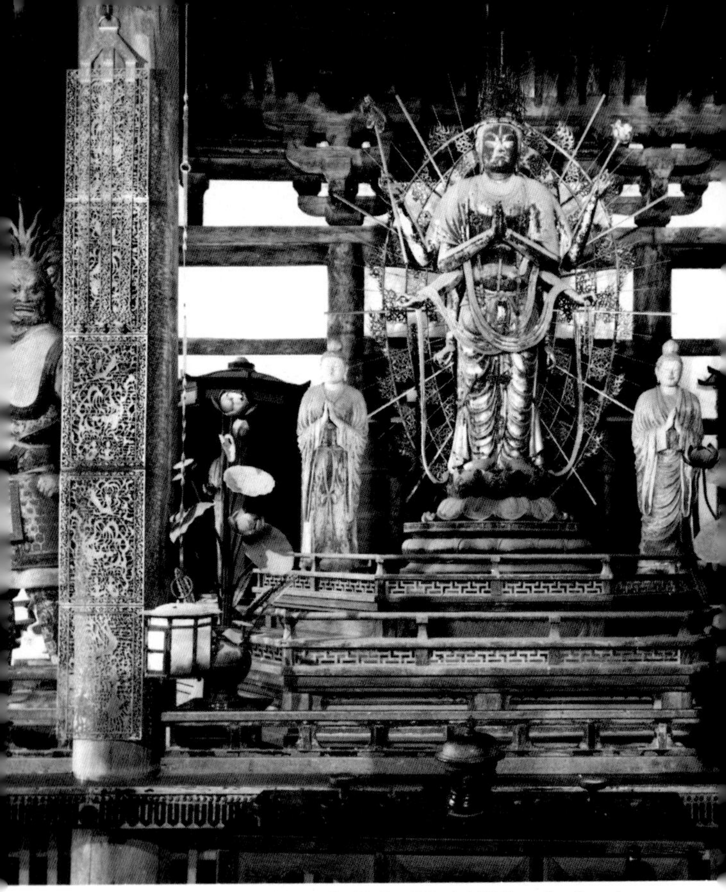

63. Interior of Sangatsudo Hall of Todai-ji Temple showing Fuku Kenjaku Kannon, Nikko Bosatsu, and Gakko Bosatsu

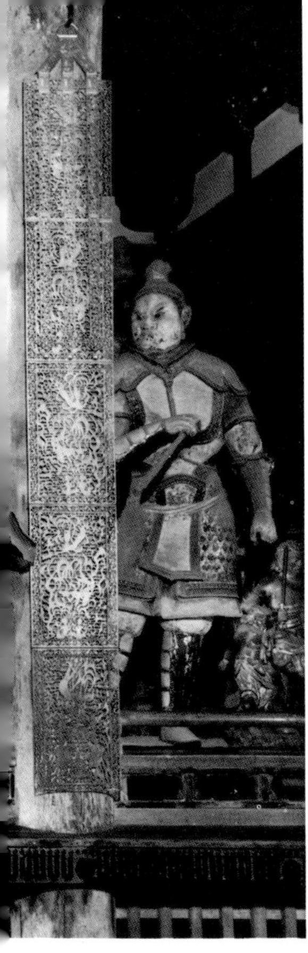

Nikko and Gakko

The bodhisattvas Nikko and Gakko are guardians of Yakushi Nyorai. Although rare, they may also appear beside Shaka or other Nyorai. Most Nikko and Gakko images present the hands folded in prayer. The two famous statues in Yakushi-ji Temple are exceptions. They are gentle in appearance and attract a great many worshippers. The Gakko image is particularly well-known in artistic and religious circles for involvement in a refurbishing argument.

The Nikko and Gakko images in Sangatsudo Hall of Todai-ji Temple are unique in several ways. First, they stand guard for Fuku Kenjyaku Kannon, not Yakushi Nyorai. Second, while the Kannon statue is effected in dry lacquer, Nikko and Gakko are done in stucco. Third, the bodhisattvas wear armor beneath their robes. These three points lead some authorities to claim the images are Bon Ten and Taishaku Ten, not Nikko and Gakko. The decisive factor that determines they are indeed Nikko and Gakko is the hands folded in prayer.

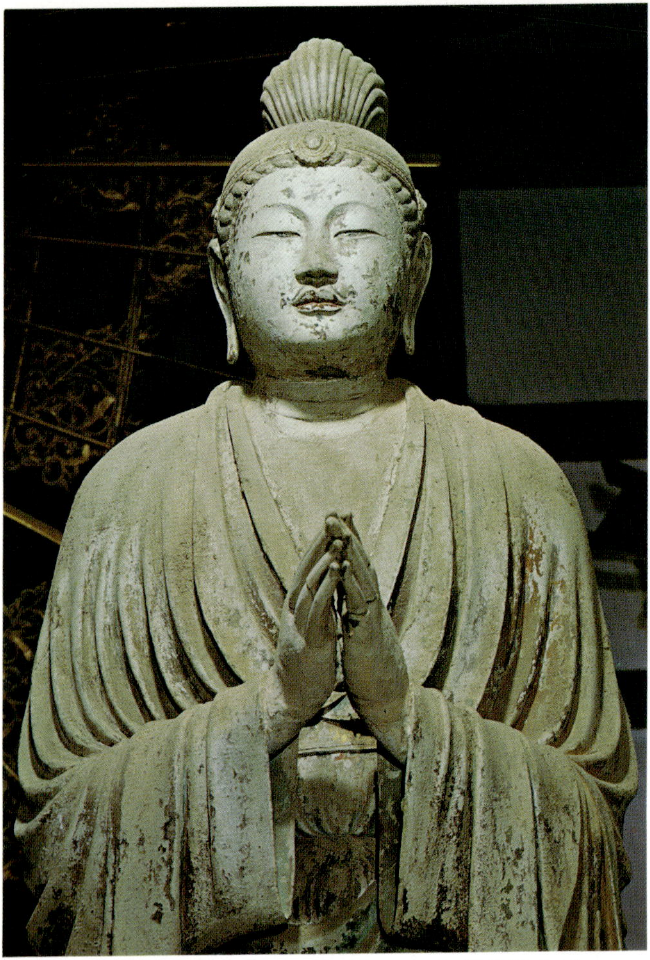

64. Nikko Bosatsu, standing; Sangatsudo Hall, Todai-ji Temple, Nara Period, Stucco, 224.7 cm

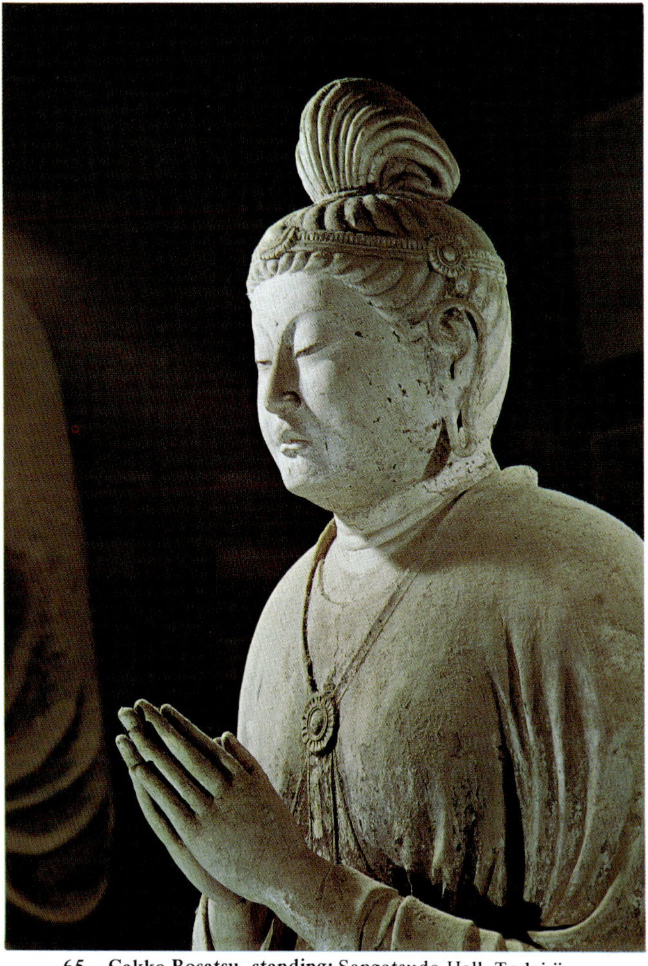

65. Gakko Bosatsu, standing; Sangatsudo Hall, Todai-ji Temple, Nara Period, Stucco, 224.8 cm

Jizo Bosatsu

The Japanese people revere and love Jizo Bosatsu as deeply as they do Kannon, and it is not uncommon to find stone Jizo images even near busy urban intersections. In fact, the words "stone buddha" alone immediately recall Jizo to many people's minds. Perhaps Jizo's popularity can be traced to the Buddhist teaching that he is commissioned to remain with and help man on earth during the "kotis of kalpa" (great many ages) between Buddha's death and Miroku's descent from Tusita. Some quarters teach that Jizo has attained buddhahood but elects to remain on earth and adopts the physical appearance of a monk. Reverence for Jizo spread especially rapidly between the twelfth and early seventeenth centuries. As might be expected, tremendous popularity has bred various superstitions concerning Jizo.

66. Jizo Bosatsu, seated;
Main Hall, Fukuchi-in Temple,
Kamakura Period, Wood,
276 cm

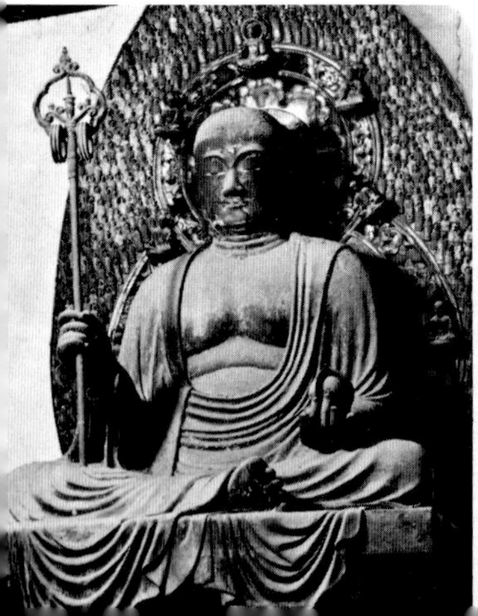

67. Jizo Bosatsu, standing;
Main Hall, Jurin-in Temple,
Kamakura Period, Stone,
147 cm

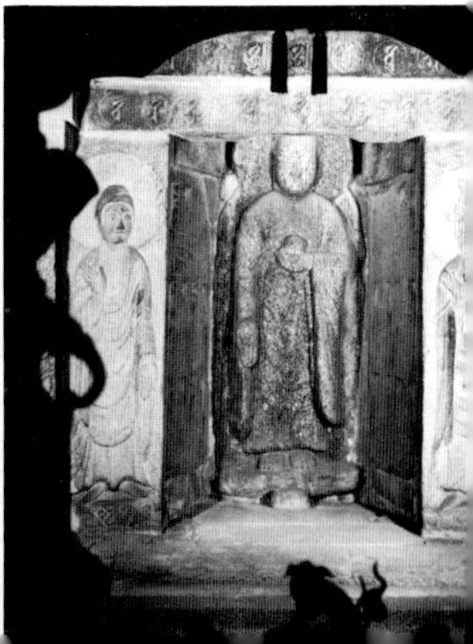

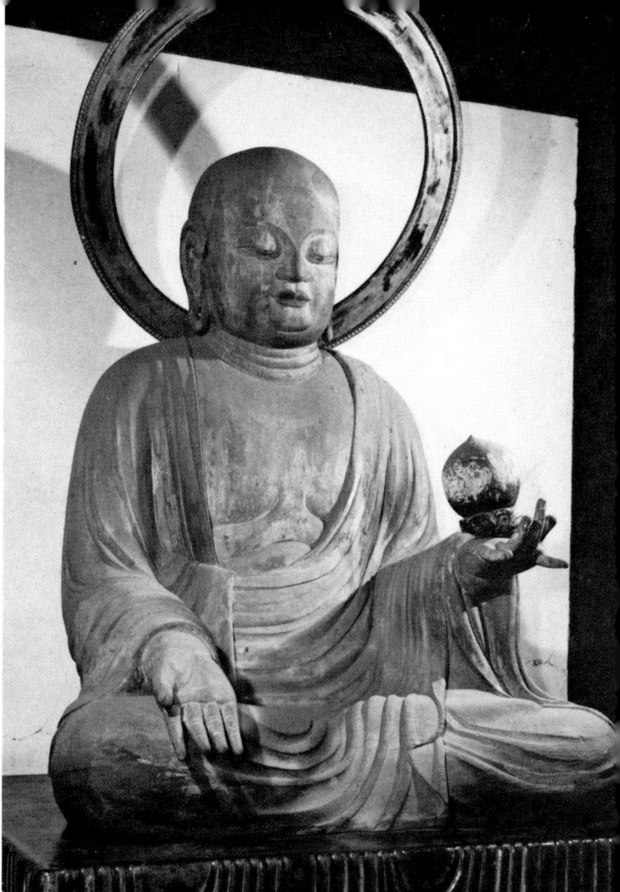

68. **Jizo Bosatsu, seated;** Lecture Hall, Koryu-ji Temple, early Heian Period, Wood, 190 cm

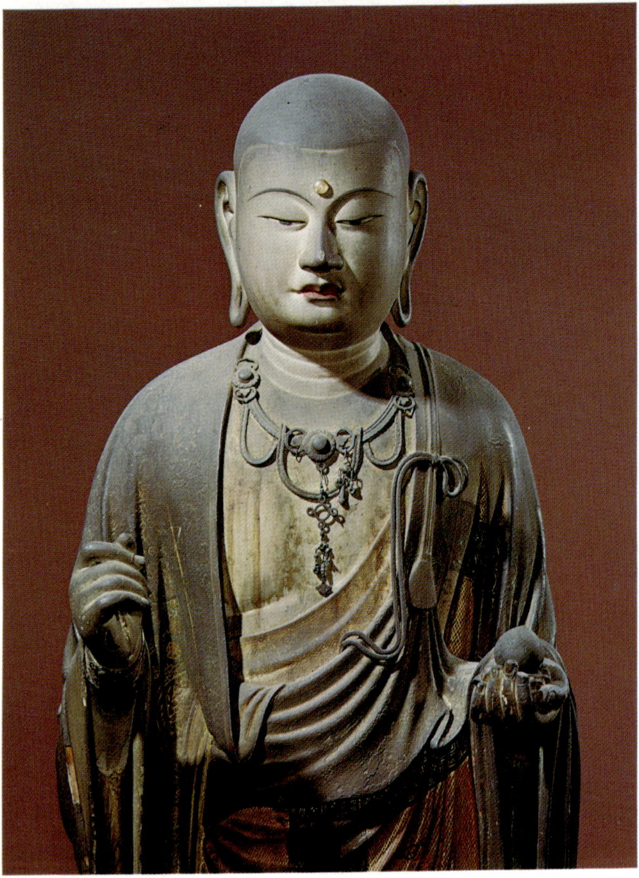

69. Jizo Bosatsu, standing; Todai-ji Temple, Kamakura Period, Wood, 91 cm

70. Kokuzo Bosatsu, standing; Horin-ji Temple, Asuka Period, Wood, 176.5 cm

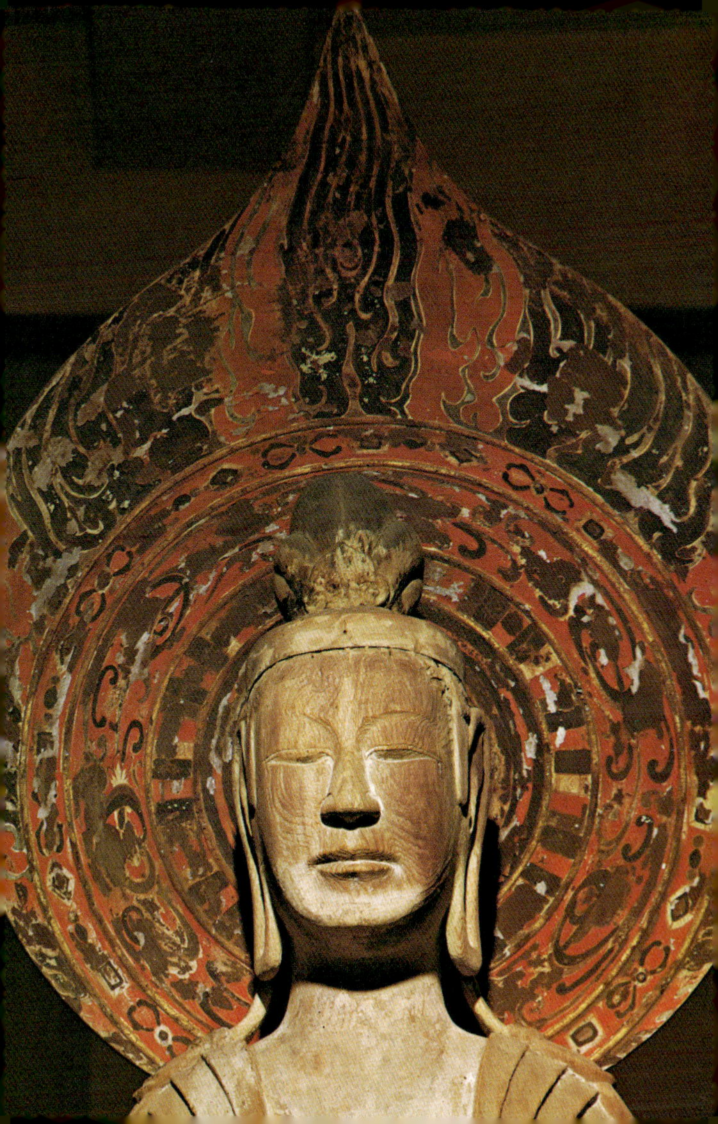

Kokuzo Bosatsu

Kokuzo Bosatsu is another bodhisattva popular among the Japanese people. His first images appeared in the eighth century. He has been prayed to for guidance and wisdom since that time. His popularity spread rapidly after the priest Kukai (774–835) returned from T'ang China in 806.

The Kokuzo image in Horin-ji Temple dates from the Asuka Period (550–650). A simple yet refined wood sculpture, it is described by some authorities as Kannon Bosatsu. The statue in Gakuan-ji Temple exhibits a rarely seen posture. Kokuzo sits on a lotus with his right leg crossed in front and his left hanging over the lotus leaf so that his foot touches the floor. The five Kokuzo images in Jingo-ji Temple date from the middle ninth century, not long after Kukai's death.

71. Godai Kokuzo Bosatsu, seated; Pagoda, Jingo-ji Temple, early Heian Period, Wood, 94.3 – 99 cm

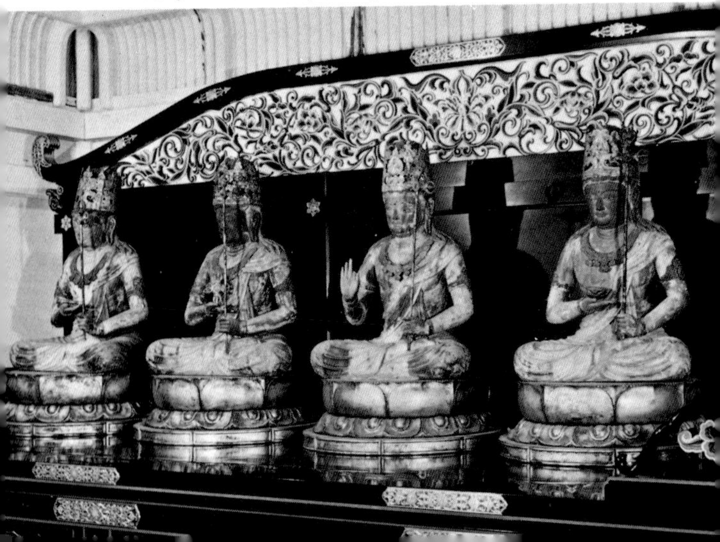

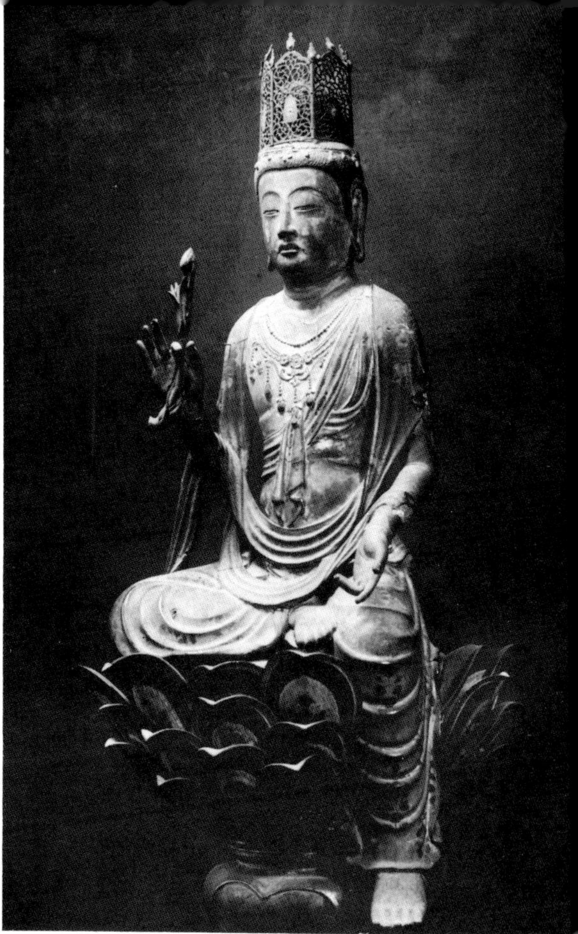

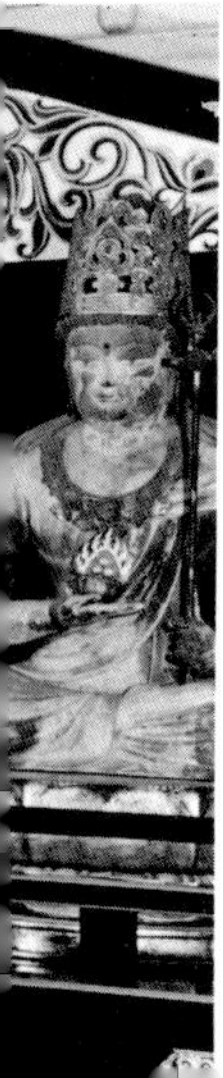

72. Kokuzo Bosatsu, half cross-legged;
Gakuan-ji Temple, Nara Period,
Dry Lacquer, 51.1 cm

Myoo

73. **Fudo Myoo, seated;** Sangatsudo Hall, Todai-ji Temple, Muromachi Period, Wood, 86 cm

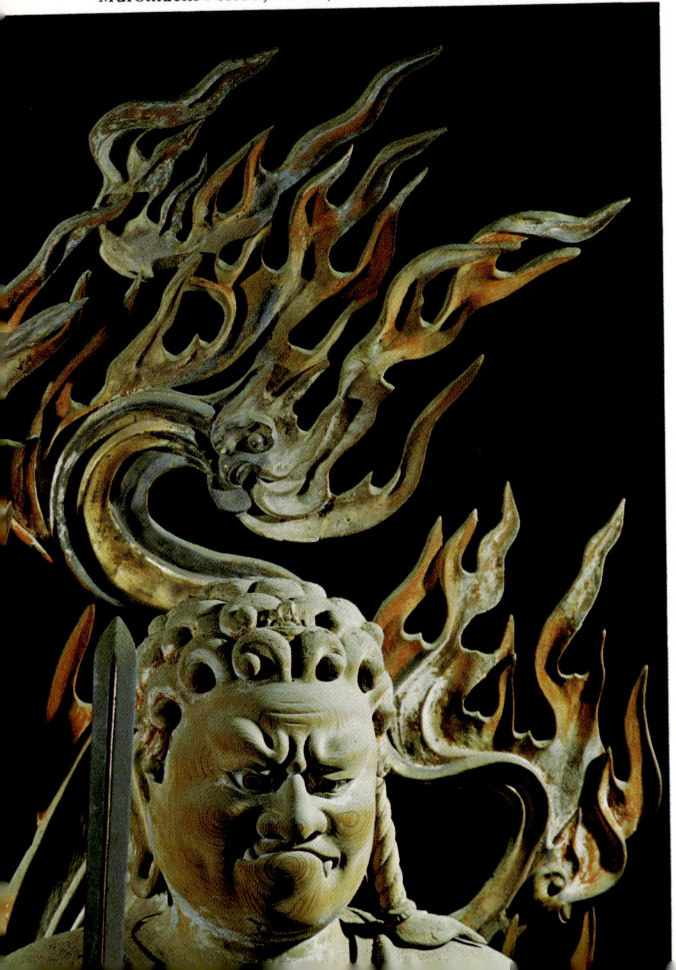

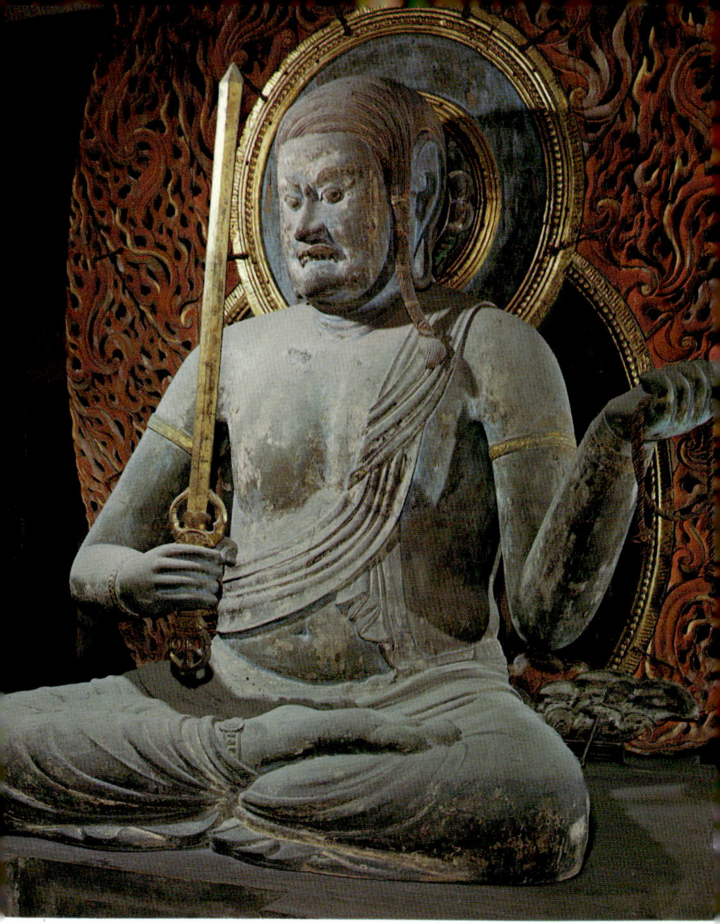

74. Fudo Myoo, seated; Lecture Hall, To-ji Temple, early Heian Period, Wood, 173.3 cm

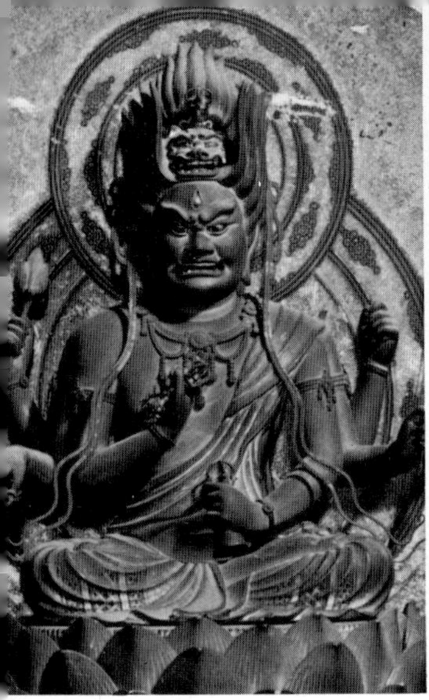

75. **Aizen Myoo, seated;**
Aizendo Hall, Saidai-ji Temple, Kamakura Period, Wood, 121.5 cm

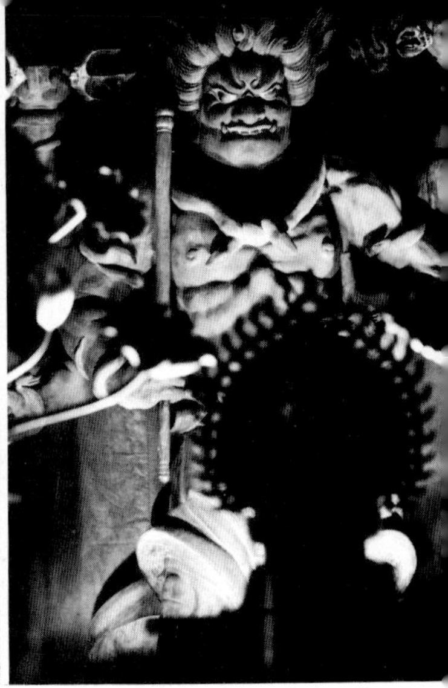

76. **Daigensui Myoo, standing;**
Akishino-dera Temple, Kamakura Period, Wood, 196.6 cm

In sharp contrast to bodhisattvas, who usually appear with gentle countenances, Myoo always exhibit fearful expressions. Besides obeying and serving Nyorai, they vanquish all evil, and lend their prodigious strength to men to help them resist temptations and overcome difficulties alon the path of religious austerities. Many men resist salvation that relies on gentle persuasion. Therein lies the significance of Myoo's existence. The best known Myoo is Fudo. Other of these so-called "fearful buddhas" are the Godai Myoo, Aizen Myoo, and Daigensui Myoo.

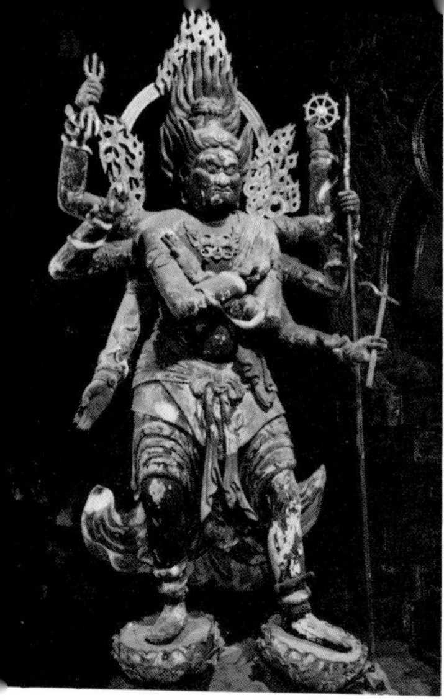

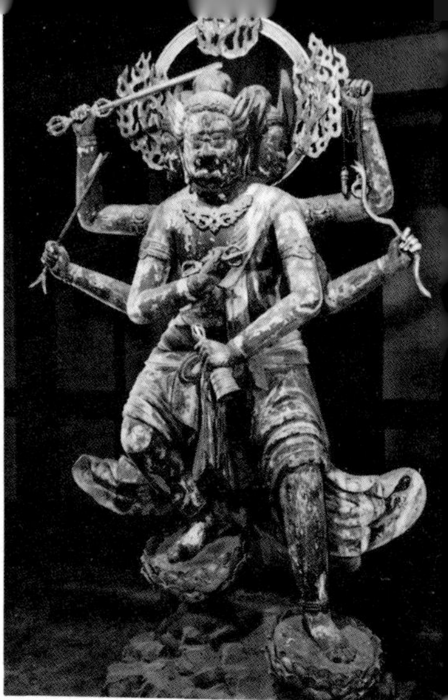

Godai Myoo, Lecture Hall, To-ji Temple, early Heian Period, Wood

▲ 77. **Gundari Myoo,** on water buffalo, 201.5 cm

◀ 78. **Kongo Yasha Myoo, standing,** 171.8 cm

▶ 79. **Daiitoku Myoo,** standing, 143.6 cm

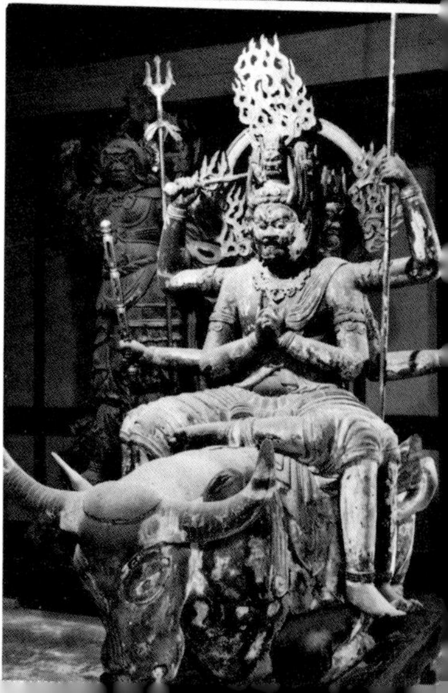

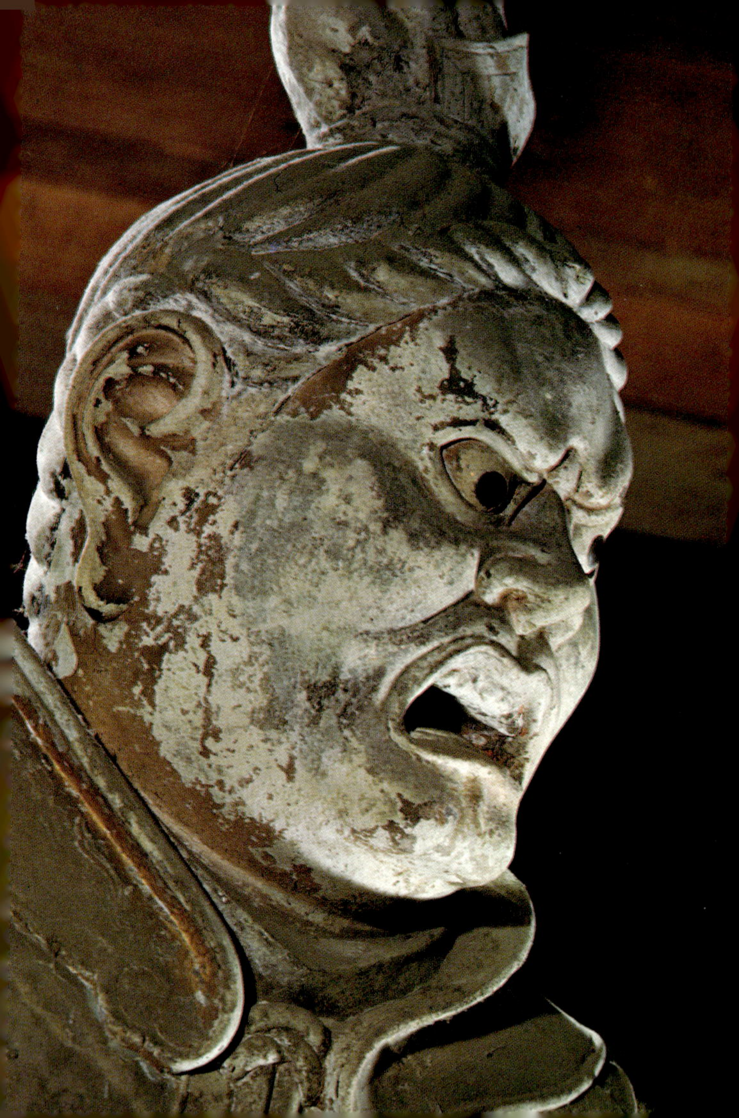

Shitenno

◀ 80.
Zocho Ten, Standing;
Kaidanin, Todai-ji Temple,
Nara Period, Stucco, 163 cm

81. ▶
Komoku Ten, standing;
Kondo Hall, Horyu-ji
Temple, Asuka Period,
Wood, 133.3 cm

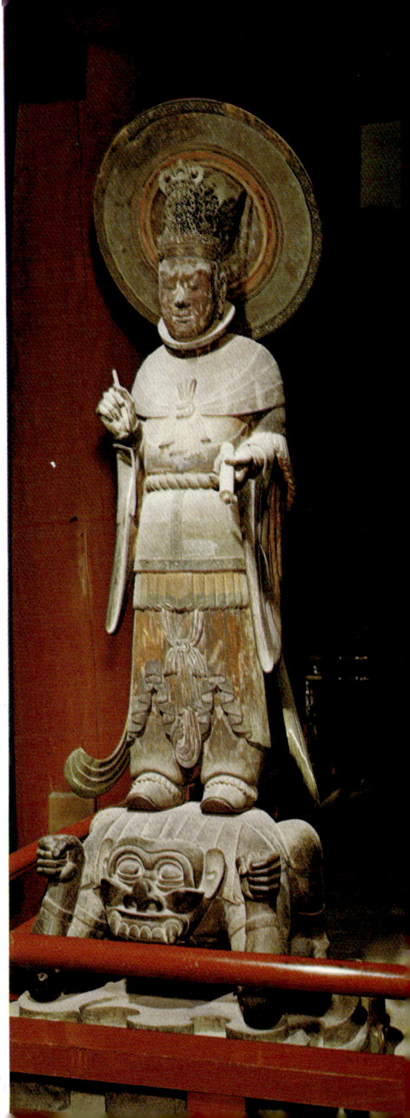

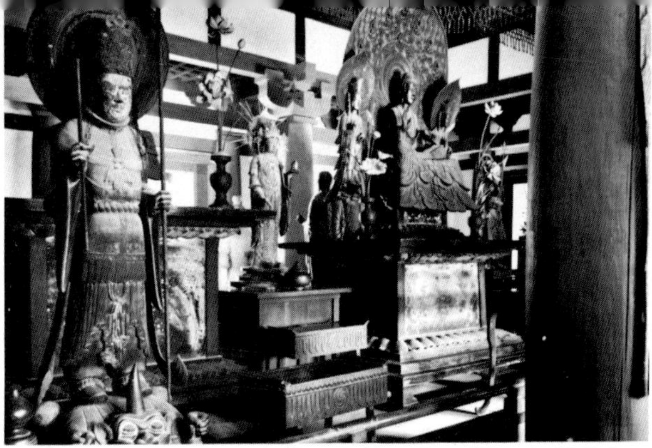

82. Zocho Ten, standing, and interior of Kondo Hall, Horyu-ji Temple, Asuka Period, Wood, 133 cm

Buddhism has borrowed gods from Brahmanism and other formal and popular religions with histories in India that predate Buddha. Myoo and Ten, for example, are former gods of folklore converted into defenders of Buddhism.

The Shitenno (Four Heavenly Kings) have been reverred for over two thousand years. They have traditionally defended the four directions surrounding the land of Buddhism: Tamon, the north; Zocho, the south; Jikoku, the east; and Komoku, the west. These Ten arrived in Japan together with Buddhism's introduction. Representative images are those in Horyu-ji Temple's Kondo Hall. They stand at the four corners of a raised dias depicting the land of Buddhism. Each Tenno stands with one foot crushing a demon beast.

Tenno were given much realistic, fearful expression from the eighth century on, and the serene composure of earlier images – such as those in Horyu-ji Temple – was replaced by a dynamic ferocity. Good examples are the Tenno images in Kaidanin of Todai-ji Temple.

83. **Zocho Ten, standing;** Kondo Hall, Taima-dera Temple, Hakuho Period, Dry lacquer, 216 cm

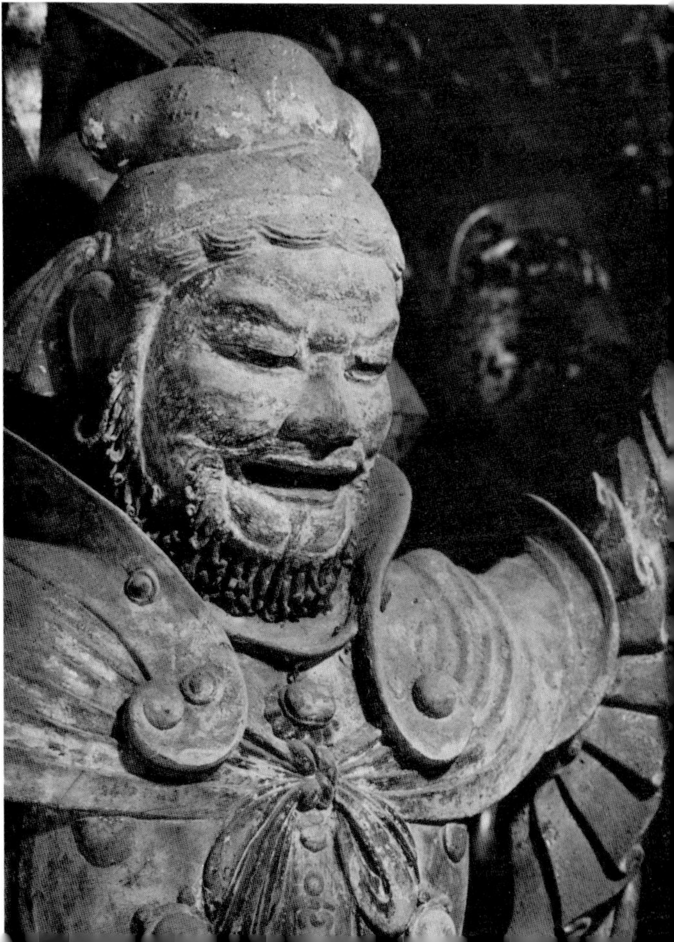

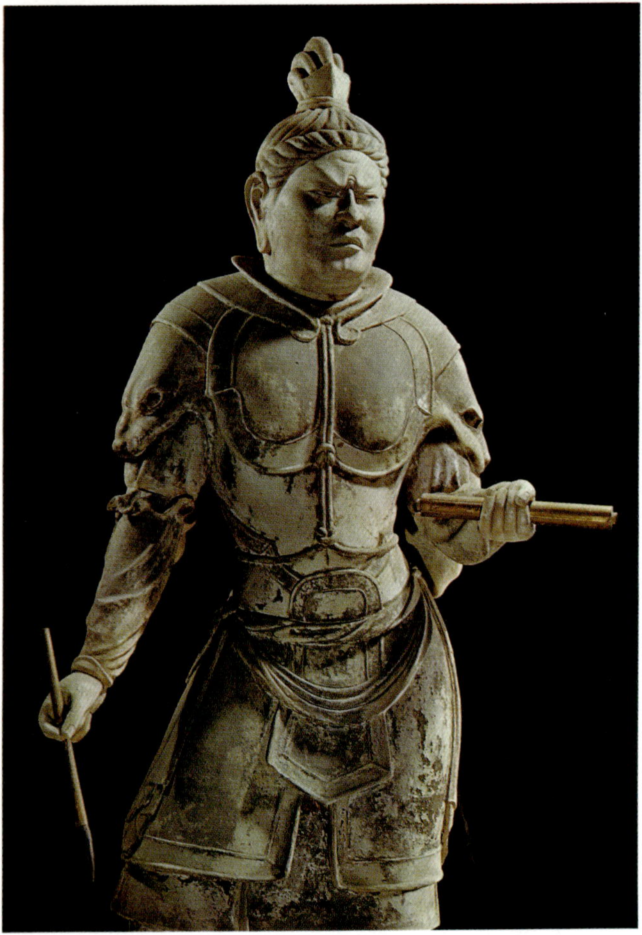

84. Komoku Ten, standing; Kaidanin, Todai-ji Temple,
Nara Period, Stucco, 162.8 cm

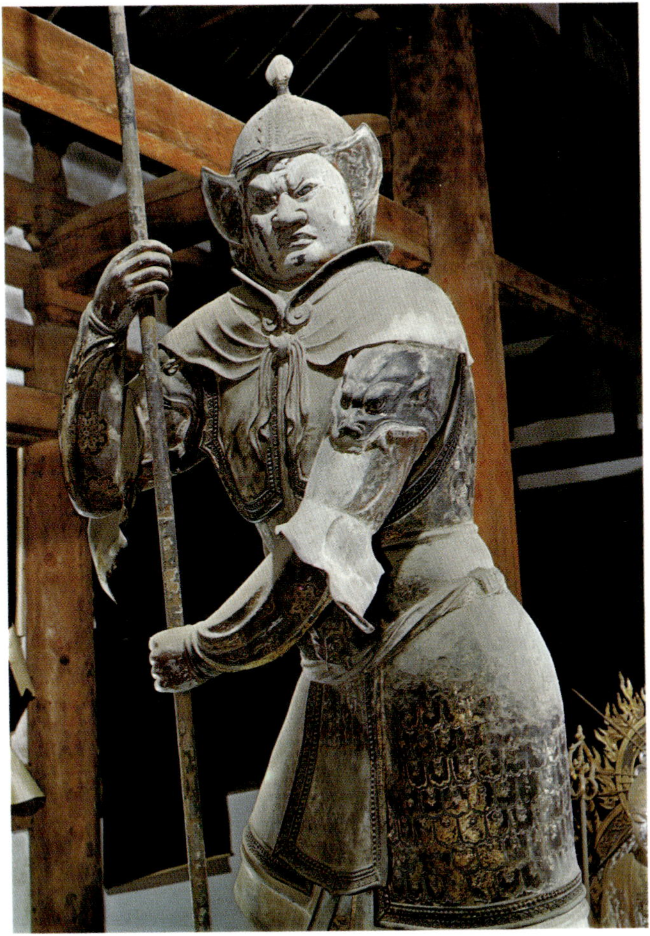

85. Zocho Ten, standing; Sangatsudo Hall, Todai-ji Temple, Nara Period, dry lacquer, 363 cm

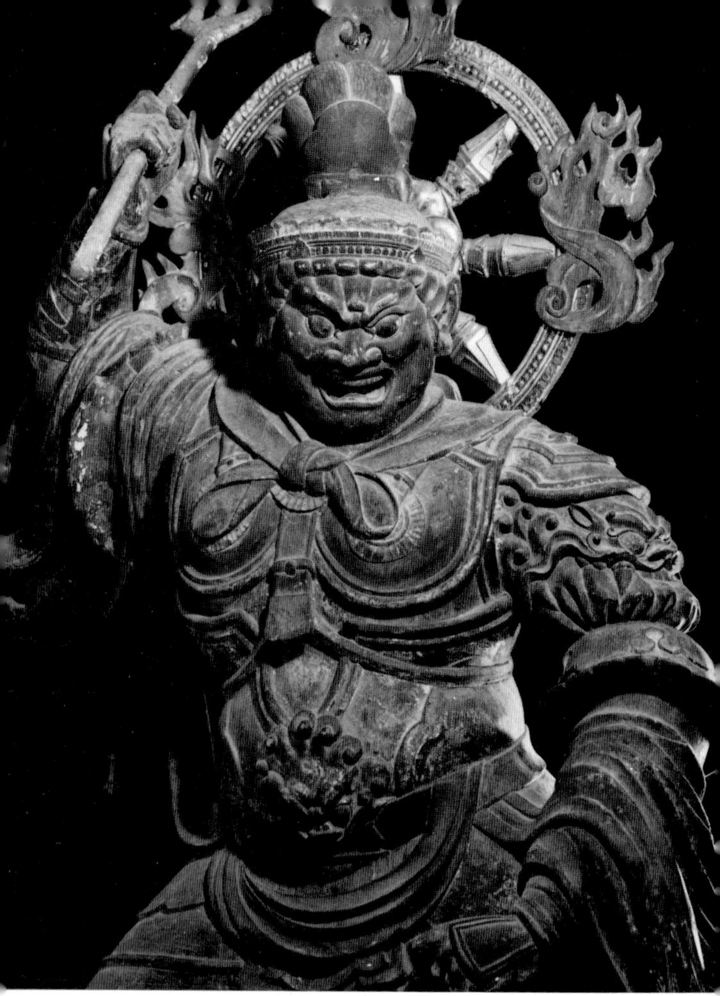

86. Jikoku Ten, standing; Lecture Hall, To-ji Temple, late Heian Period, Wood, 183 cm

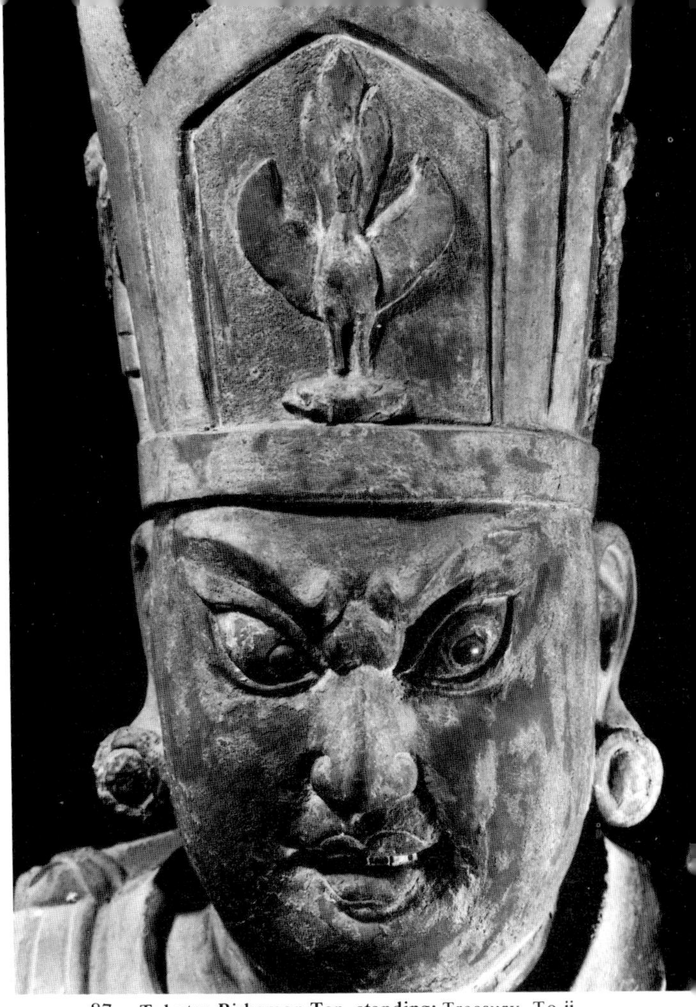

87. **Tobatsu Bishamon Ten, standing;** Treasury, To-ji Temple, T'ang Period, Wood, 206.3 cm

88. Bon Ten and Kongo Rikishi, standing; Sangatsudo Hall, Todai-ji Temple, Nara Period, Dry lacquer, Bon Ten 403 cm, Kongo Rikishi 332 cm

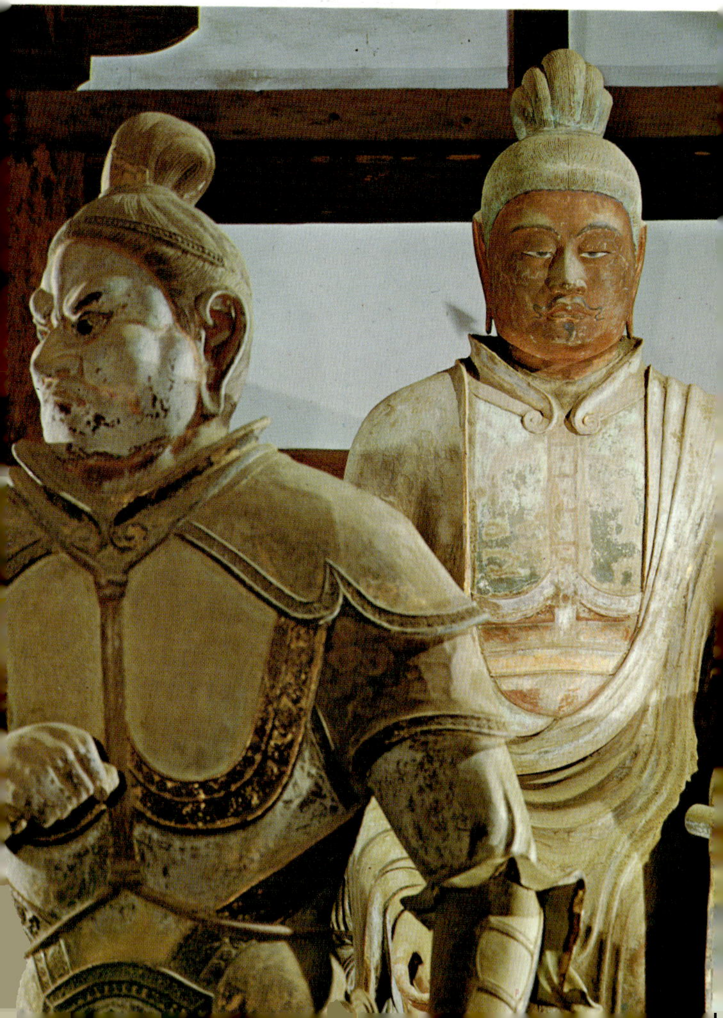

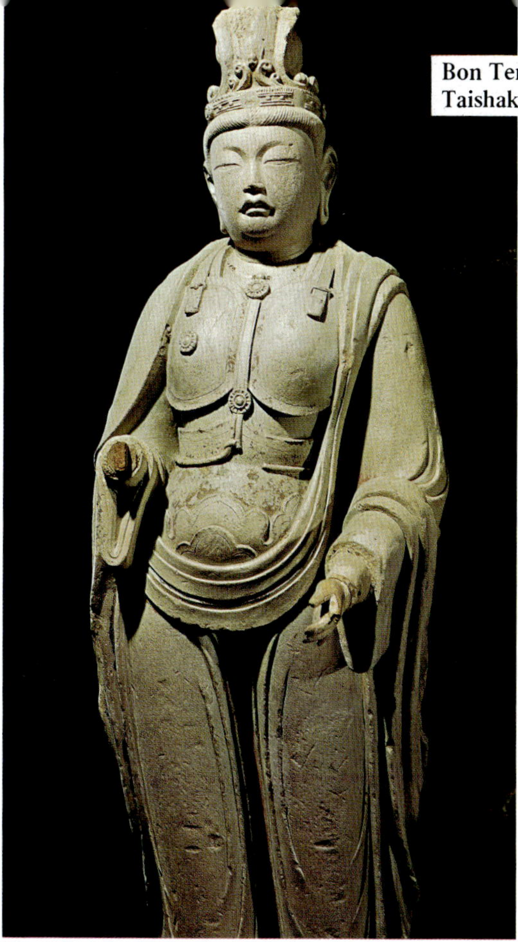

89. Bon Ten, standing;
Hozoden Treasury, Horyu-ji Temple,
Nara Period, Stucco, 110.2 cm

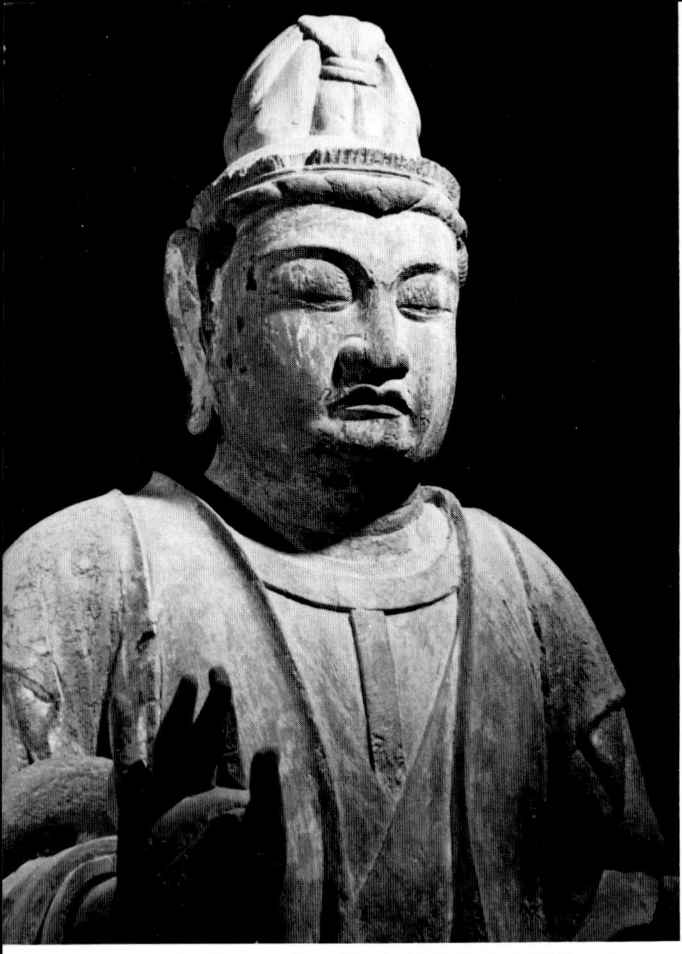

90. Taishaku Ten, standing; Kondo Hall, Toshodai-ji Temple, Nara Period, Wood, 206 cm

Bon Ten and Taishaku Ten defend the land of Buddhism and Shaka's world at a higher level than the Shitenno. The stucco images of these two Ten standing in Horyu-ji Temple's dining area are especially old and noteworthy works of art. They display armor under long-sleeved Chinese-style garments. Despite their gentle countenances the Ten still express a severity befitting their station.

The wooden images in Toshodai-ji Temple's Kondo Hall also wear armor beneath their garments. The Taishaku Ten image in To-ji Temple is a masterpiece of esoteric Buddhist sculpture.

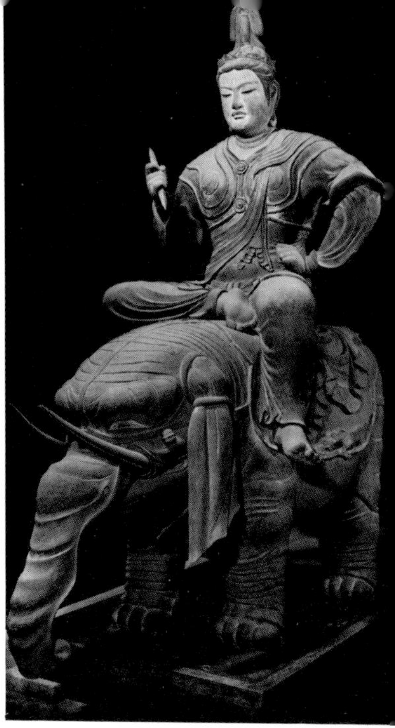

91. Taishaku Ten, seated; Lecture Hall, To-ji Temple, early Heian Period, Wood, 100.4 cm

92. Kongo Rikishi, standing; Nandaimon Gate, Todai-ji Temple, ▶ Kamakura Period, Wood, 8.03 m

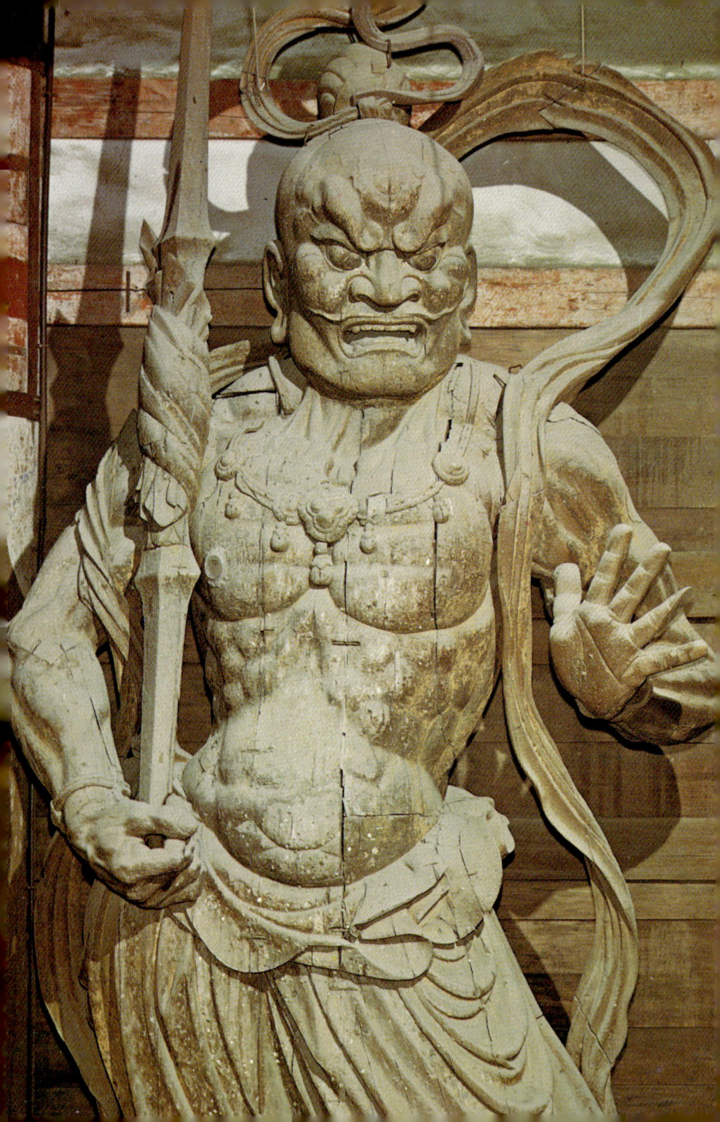

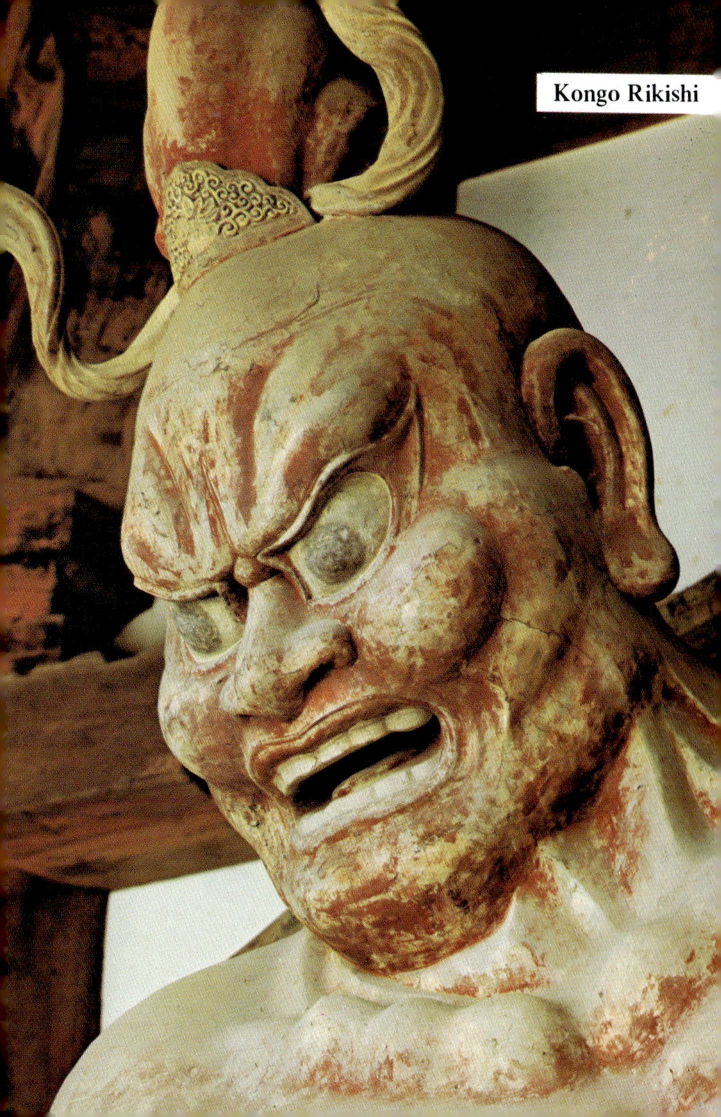

Kongo Rikishi

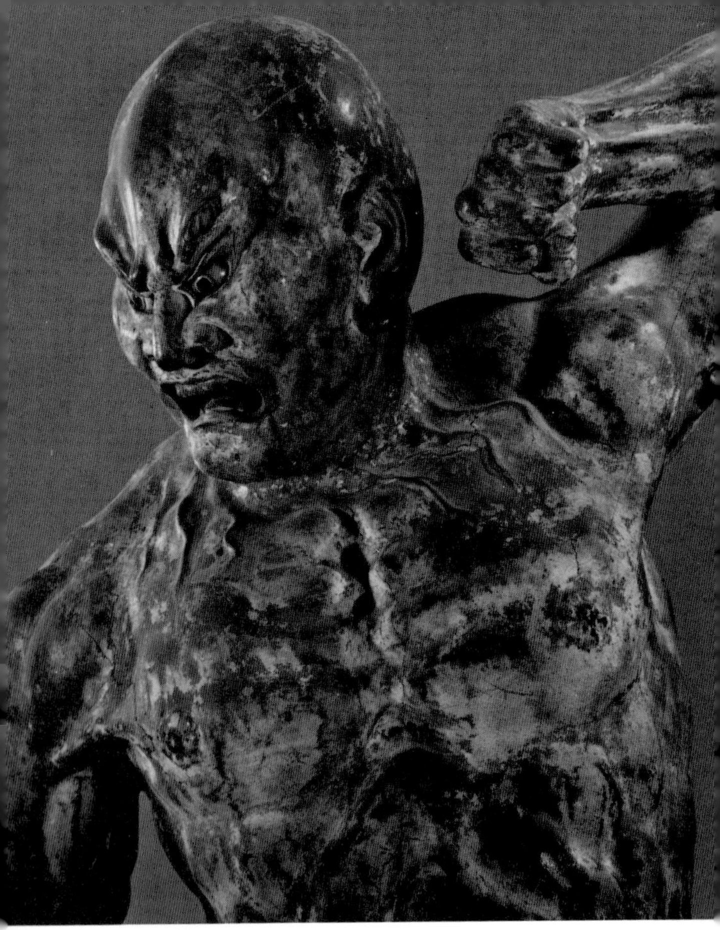

93. **Kongo Rikishi, standing;** Treasury, Kofuku-ji Temple, Kamakura Period, Wood, 161 cm

◀ 94. **Kongo Rikishi, standing;** Chumon Gate, Horyu-ji Temple, Nara Period, Stucco, 378.8 cm

Kongo Rikishi is the traditional guardian of Buddhist temple gates, and some extant images date from the eighth century. A strong, muscular figure, often with ogre-like facial features, Kongo Rikishi guards both sides of a gate – one image on each side. Because there are two guardians at every gate, Kongo Rikishi is popularly called Nio (literally, two kings). The Nio guarding Horyu-ji Temple's Chumon Gate date from 711, which makes them the oldest Kongo Rikishi images in Japan. The right-hand (facing the gate) image is an open-mouthed type, and is vermilion-colored; the left-hand image is a closed-mouth type, and is charcoal-colored. Both are made of stucco. Todai-ji Temple's Nandaimon Gate Nio are Japan's largest. They were created by Unkei and his disciples and exemplify the realism of Kamakura period sculpture.

95. Kongo Rikishi, standing; Nandaimon Gate, Todai-ji Temple, Kamakura Period, Wood, 8.03 m

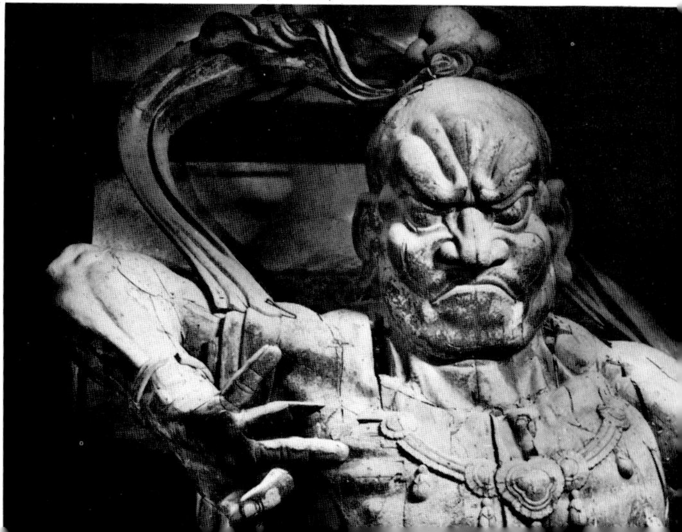

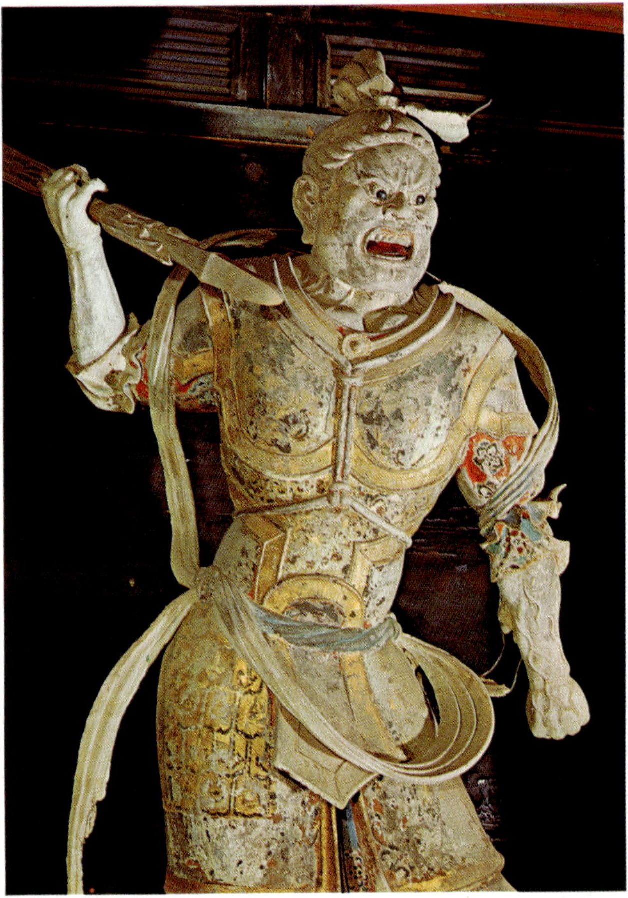

96. Shukongoshin, standing; Sangatsudo Hall, Todai-ji Temple, Nara Period, Stucco, 173.9 cm

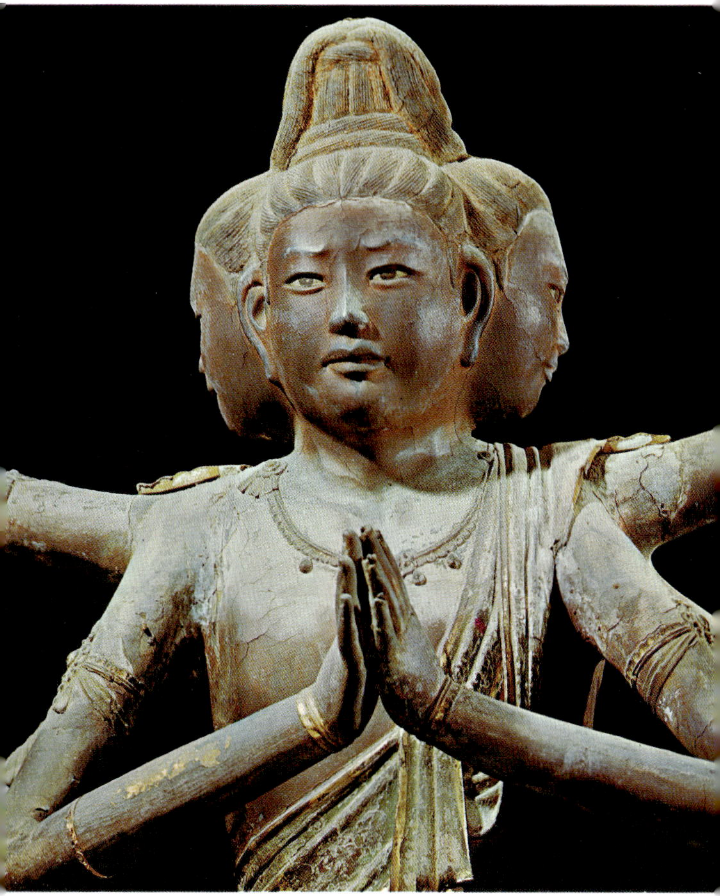

97. Ashura, standing; Treasury, Kofuku-ji Temple, Nara Period, Dry lacquer, 153.1 cm

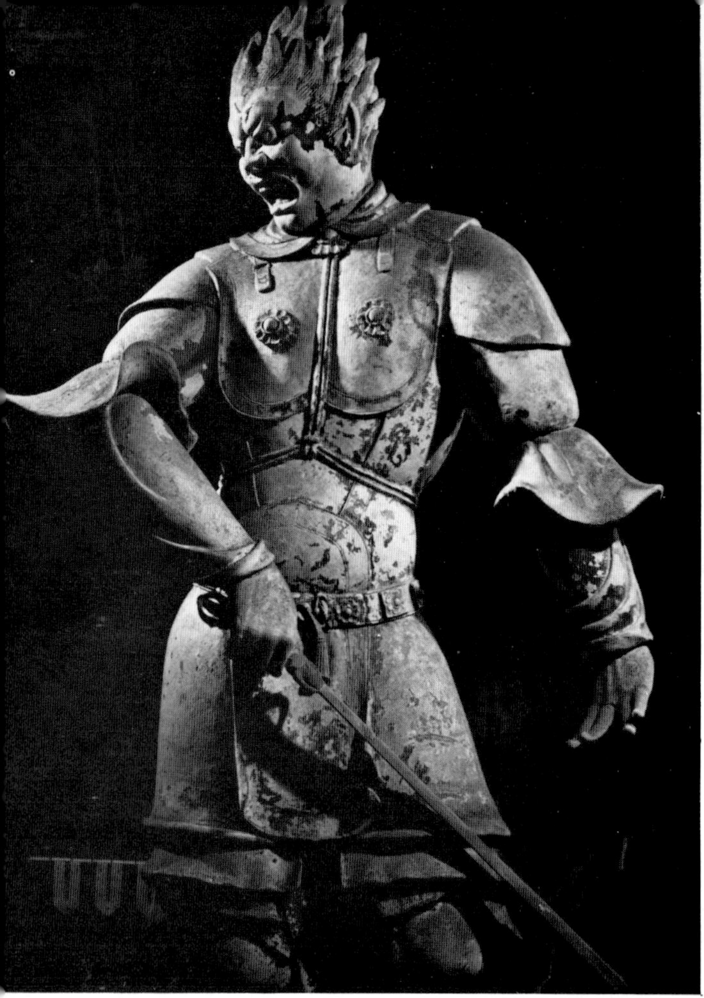

98. **Basara Daisho, standing;** Main Hall, Shin Yakushi-ji Temple, Nara Period, Stucco, 166.1 cm

Juni Jinsho

The Juni Jinsho (Twelve Heavenly Generals) attend to Yakushi Nyorai. As seen in Shin Yakushi-ji Temple's Kondo Hall, the twelve Jinsho are fierce warriors suited in armor who surround and protect Yakushi. Tradition holds that the Jinsho divide the day into two twelve-hour periods with each warrior standing watch one hour in day and one at night. After the twelfth century the Juni Jinsho acquired associations with the twelve zodiacal signs. The particular sign is found on the image's crown or headpiece.

99. Interior of Main Hall of Shin Yakushi-ji Temple showing Yakushi Nyorai and Juni Jinsho

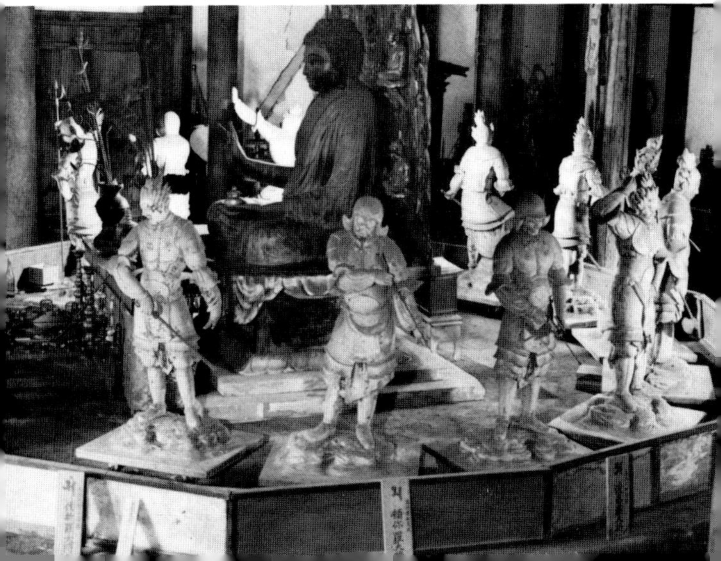

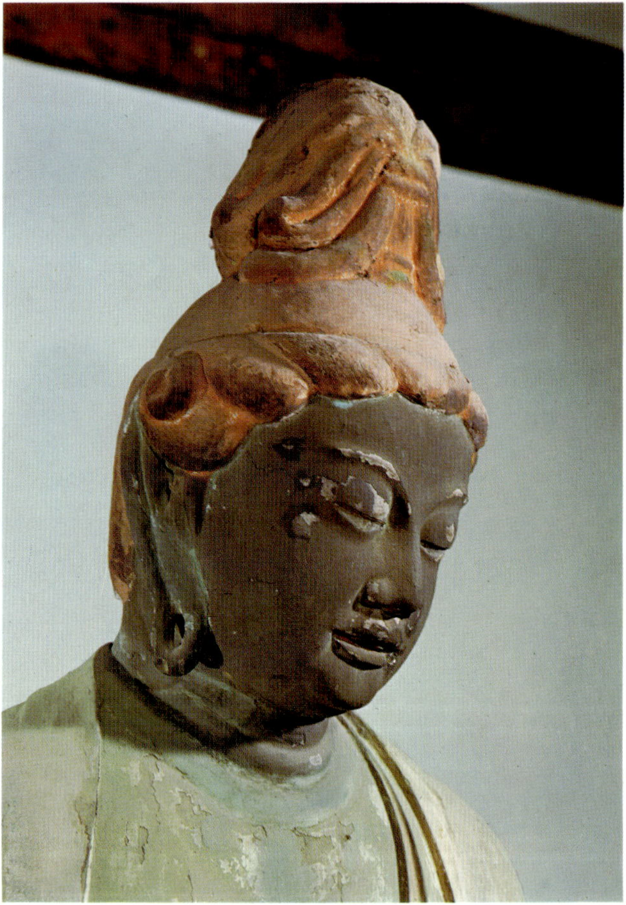

100. Gigei Ten, standing; Main Hall, Akishino-dera Temple, Nara Period, Dry lacquer, 212 cm

101. Kissho Ten, standing; Main Hall, Joruri-ji Temple, Kamakura Period, Wood, 90 cm

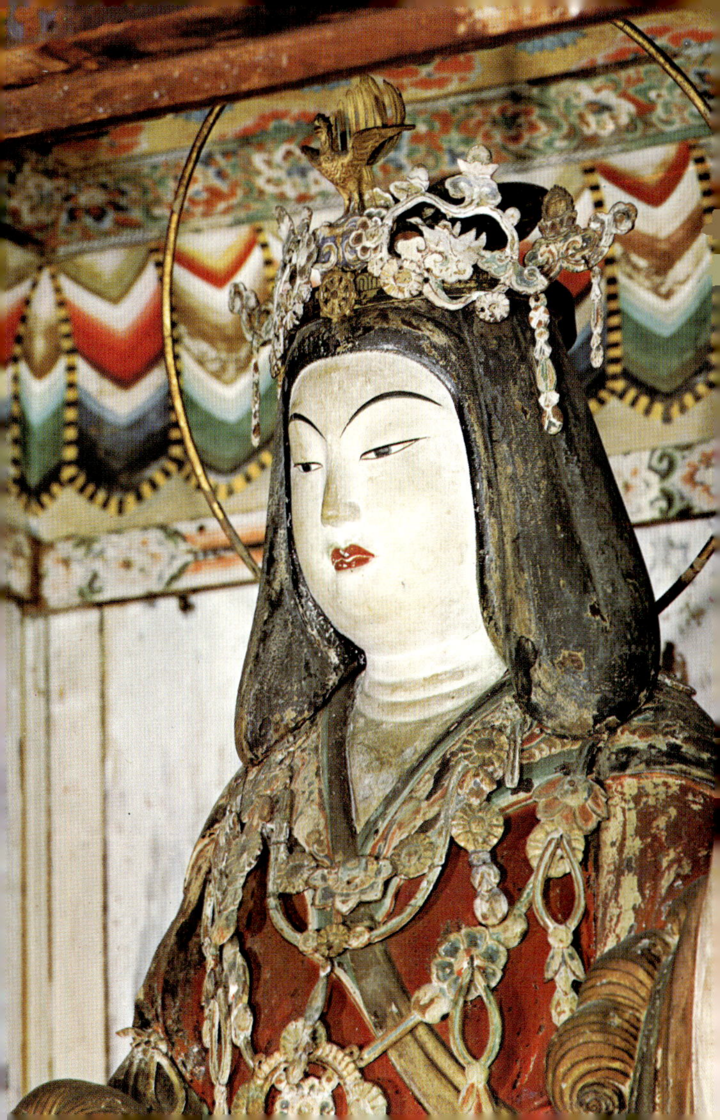

Tennyo

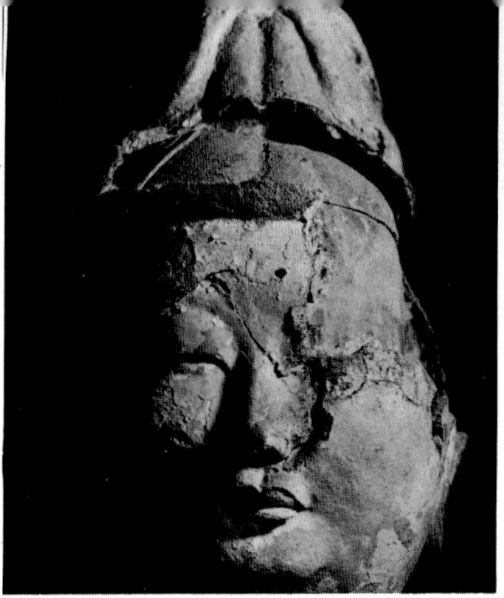

102. Benzai Ten, standing; Sangatsudo Hall, Todai-ji Temple, Nara Period, Stucco, 218.7 cm

The Ten of Buddhism are not always fearful males. Beautiful Ten like Kissho, Benzai and Gigei are generally depicted with soft, fleshy figures. Kissho Ten has been reverred since the eighth century. She promises happiness, prosperity and abundant harvests. The stucco Kissho image in Todai-ji Temple's Sangatsudo Hall and Yakushi-ji Temple's Kissho painting both date from the T'ang period and depict the classical female beauty of the age. Joruri-ji Temple's statue of Kissho Ten is a representative Kamakura Period masterpiece.

Benzai Ten is the goddess of plentiful water. The Benzai image in Sangatsudo Hall of Todai-ji Temple is one of Japan's oldest, but is badly disfigured and in need of repair. Gigei Ten is the goddess of the arts. The Gigei image in Akishino-dera Temple is particularly well-known.

103. Kissho Ten, standing; Sangatsudo Hall, Todai-ji Temple, Nara Period, Stucco, 201.9 cm

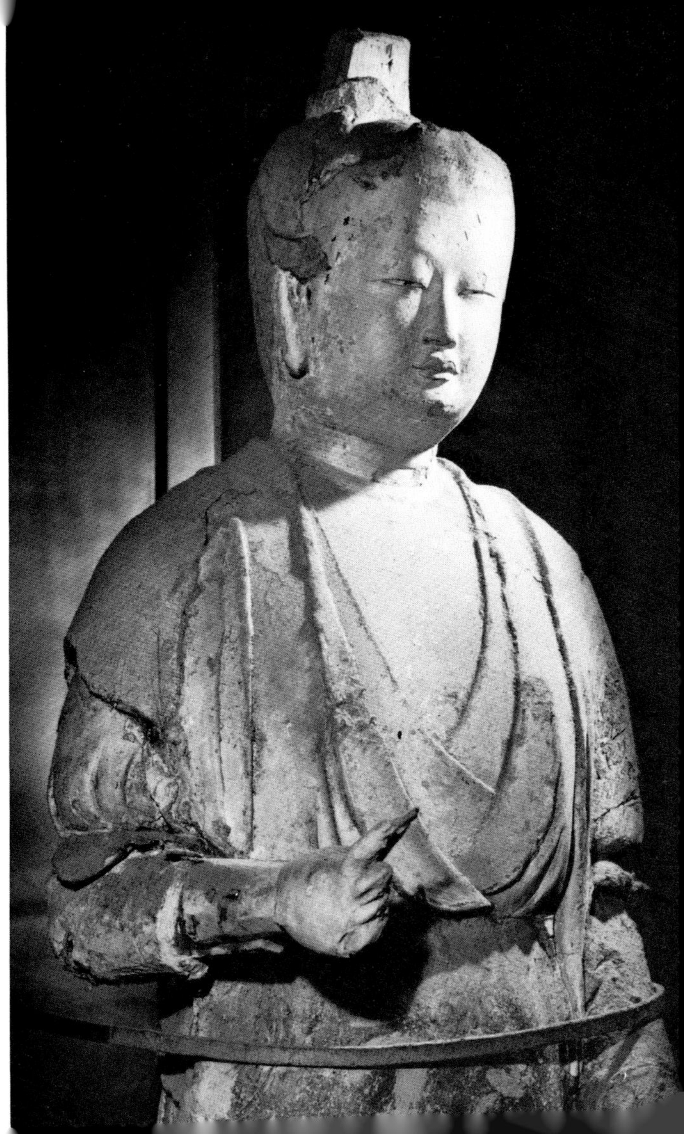

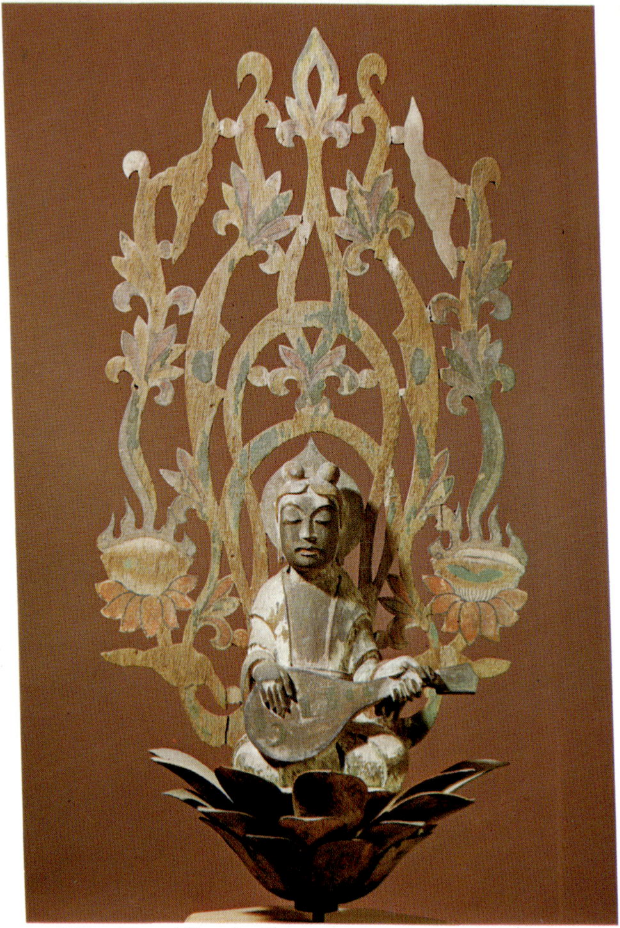

104. Tengai Tennin, Hozoden Treasury, Horyu-ji Temple, Asuka Period, Wood, 17 cm

From the Authors

While Buddhism as a religion is said to be in dangerous decline, Buddhist art – particularly Buddhist images – has never in history enjoyed the tremendous popular appreciation it does today. One wonders what reasons explain the religious decline and artistic prosperity of Buddhism, and what the present trend bodes for the future.

The "boom" in Buddhist art appreciation suggests to some Buddhist priests the possibility that through the art people may become active in the religion. Some priests, therefore, have stepped to the forefront to help the layman understand Buddhist images. Others accept without complaint their role as simple caretakers in temples housing National Treasures.

As we realized Buddhist art appreciation really was growing, we discussed what we might do as so-called "experts." After much talk, we decided to present in book form and in layman's language the basic knowledge necessary to understand Buddhist images. Rather than an expensive tome that only a selected stratum of society could afford, we hoped to publish an easy-to-obtain book that in content would be as rich as higher priced volumes.

We invite our readers to unshackle themselves from an overrationalized reality, to abandon themselves completely to glorious sentimentalism, and then to raise themselves up again to where they can look serenely at Buddhist images with an appreciative eye.

This book's purpose, and the wish of both authors, is that the reader may find in Buddhist images or Buddhist thought something of value, some contemporary significance that will help him with personal problems.

I. VIEWING BUDDHIST IMAGES

Recent years have witnessed a marked increased in popular interest in Japan's cultural properties, particularly in Buddhist art objects. Buddhist images in the temples of Kyoto and Nara attract hordes of visitors throughout the year. The pleasant spring and autumn months are most crowded, but even summer's heat and winter's cold fail to dim the current fervor.

The "Buddhas" that visitors view, however, are not all Buddhas. Some are bodhisattvas, others are heavenly guardians, attendants, or other deities in the Buddhist pantheon. "Buddha" has become an inclusive term referring to the various sculptures (and paintings) whose common characteristic is their connection with Buddhism. A more fitting term for these sculptures is perhaps "Buddhist images." The images are multitudinous and even the practiced viewer experiences difficulty making and understanding the distinctions among them.

Some quarters question the value of distinctions, believing that the ability to differentiate between a Buddha and a bodhisattva is secondary to appreciating the image as an artistic achievement. But in Buddhist art, as in all religious art, certain details – hand position, clothing style, hair style, objects carried – symbolize fundamental religious ideals and long-standing traditions. The artist is ever aware of these. A Buddhist sculptor creating a triad fully recognizes the inter-relationship of the central figure, the supporting figures – usually one at each side – and the viewer, and his cognizance gains expression in his creation. If the viewer cannot identify the figures or realize the various relationships in a triad, he misses both the religious significance and considerable of the artistic meaning. Familiarity with the iconography involved certainly enhances one's appreciation of most religious art. Such familiarity is especially desirable to have when temple-viewing in Japan, where the profusion of religious sculpture will guarantee exhausted confusion for the wholly uninitiated.

After noting an image's identifying details, one will then step back to appreciate the figure in general terms. Too much emphasis on iconography will blind the viewer to the importance of the whole, and only when contemplating the whole image does one experience its full religious and artistic impact. This impact is represented by the feelings evoked in Basho's haiku.

> The chrysanthemum smell –
> In the old town of Nara,
> Many ancient Buddhas.

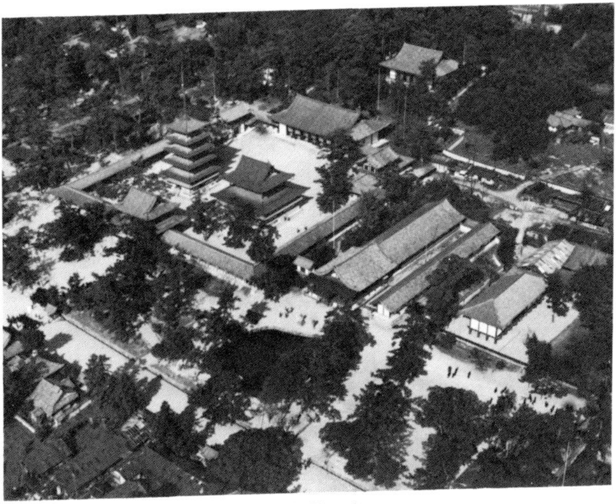

Horyu-ji Temple

II. THE BEGINNINGS OF BUDDHIST ART IN JAPAN

Scholars still argue about the date of Buddhism's arrival in Japan. Japan maintained contacts with the Korean Peninsula and China from at least the fifth century, and knowledge of Buddhism probably entered the country during Emperor Keitai's reign (507 – 531 A.D.). Since there was an influx of immigrants about that time, the newcomers likely brought their religion with them and continued to practice it in the new setting. Japan's formal introduction to Buddhism, however, came in Imperial Era 1212, or A.D. 552. "One, two, one, two, Over the seas from Kudara they came . . ." is a Japanese ditty recited for remembering the date when Kudara's (Paekche in old Korea) King Syong-myong sent envoys bearing sutras and a Buddhist image to Japan's Emperor Kimmei. This Shaka image was presented to Soga no Iname, who promptly installed it in the Asuka Mukawara residence.

Soga's action enraged the Mononobe clan, and the two families clashed frequently in the sixth century over the Buddhist question. The Soga favored accepting Buddhist teachings; the more conservative Mononobe demanded Buddhism's exclusion on the grounds that it undermined' Shinto, the indigenous religion. By the early seventh century, pro-Buddhist forces prevailed. Japan thus entered the Asuka Period, years that were to be colored throughout by Buddhist thought and art. Japanese by this time were creating original Buddha images, mostly of Shaka.

Shaka, the historical Buddha, was born Gautama Siddartha, the prince of Kapila, in 551 B.C. in central India. This was twenty years earlier than the birth of the great Greek philosopher Pythagoras. After attaining enlightenment, the Buddha preached and explained the doctrines of Buddhism until his peaceful death (the paranirvana) at the age of eighty. In the fifty century B.C. Japan was still in the Jomon stage, and had a hunting and fishing culture. The rice-growing, agricultural

Yayoi Period did not begin until nearly two hundred years after Buddha's death.

Shaka's remains were cremated according to Indian practice. His disciples reverenced the bones not cremated, called *shari*, believing they evidenced Shaka's liberation from the wheel of worldy existence and entrance into permanent Buddhahood. They divided the *shari* among themselves, carried them to their respective home regions, and built *stupa* – mound-shaped graves of earth – to house them. Together with Buddhism's export, *stupa* developed in some countries into multi-storied pagodas. Since Buddhists considered *stupa* the most sacred places of worship, great attention to detail marked their construction and many magnificent structures were erected. Even today one sees *stupa* remains throughout India.

The Sanchi and Buddha-gaya *stupa*, great earthern knolls built over stone foundations, are particularly famous. Sculpted illustrations of the Jataka stories (tales of the Buddha's life), scenes from the Lotus Sutra, and arabesques decorate the stone foundations. Considered too magnificent to be expressed in human form, Shaka is sculpted symbolically as the Wheel of the Law, the Footprint, the Jeweled Throne, and a great bodhi-tree.

The early years following Buddha's death constituted an aniconic period: no Buddhist images existed, only *stupa* housing the *shari*. Thus, the *stupa* was the original Buddhist art form. Artists did not begin to produce Buddha images until two hundred years after Shakamuni's death, around the time of King Ashoka. The iconic art developed along with *stupa* construction from the third to the first centuries B.C.

Numerous images representing early Buddhist art remain in India's Gandhara region in the Northwest. Alexander the Great extended his empire to this area, and Gandharan artisans incorporated many Greek elements into their sculpture. When Buddhism reached Gandhara, Greco-Buddhist images made their first appearance. Today, many Greco-Buddhist style sculptures are excavated in the region. Most are strangely Occidental Buddhas, with beards, full moustaches, and wavey rather than tightly-curled hair. These Western-style figures stimulated artists to develop other Buddhist sculptural styles, and each region eventually expressed its own artistic interpretation of the Shaka figure. Image worship thus gradually achieved a status in Buddhism alongside *shari* worship.

Buddhism travelled the silk routes of Central Asia to reach China around the first or second century A.D. Two particularly fine Buddhist works in China are the Northern Wei Dynasty Buddhist caves at Tun-huang in Kansu, and Yun-kang in Shansi Province. New art forms suitable to Chinese topography and temperament developed as Buddhism spread throughout the country. From China, the Korean Peninsula made a natural bridge to Japan.

The Asuka Daibutsu – Japan's First Buddhist Image: When Soga no Iname converted a residence into a temple in 552 to house the Buddhist image received from Korea's King Syongmyong, the conservative Mononobe clan was enraged at the respect shown a foreign religious image. Mononobe proclaimed Soga's action heretical and caused the Buddhist image to be thrown into the Naniwa Canal. This initiated bloody disputes between the Soga and Mononobe families over Buddhism which raged for almost fifty years.

In 588, Emperor Sushun's first year of reign, Soga no Umako ordered Asuka-ji Temple's construction to house *shari* received from Kudara (Paekche, Korea). The temple was completed in 596, the fourth year of Emperor Suiko. In 605, the Emperor issued an edict to his counsellors and high government officials ordering a large bronze Buddha to be erected. This was the Asuka Daibutsu, a fifty-three-foot high bronze image of Shaka Nyorai installed in Asuka-ji Temple's Ango-in. The Asuka Daibutsu evidenced the final, full acceptance of Buddhism in Japan.

The master craftsman Tori Busshi supervised the huge Buddha's construction. Tori was the descendant of generations of devout Buddhists. His grandfather was Shiba Tatto, an immigrant from the state of Southern Liang in China. Tatto arrived in Japan around 522, and began secretly spreading

Buddhist doctrine thirty years before Buddhism's formal introduction into the country. Some reports indicate that Tatto brought relics with him from China. At any rate, he obtained land and settled in Yamato, and he and his family maintained their religious beliefs. Tori's father, Tasuna, entered the priesthood to pray for the successful convalescence of the Emperor Yomei (586 – 7), and one of Tori's aunts was the first Japanese nun. Tori himself joined the prestigious Saddlemakers Guild, originally a group of saddlemakers who later became known for their high quality Buddhist craftsmanship. Tori was also a skilled engineer.

Even the sophisticated court nobles were suprised at the Asuka Daibutsu's success. The casting itself was masterful, but so also was installment in the large hall previously built to house the image. Tori's workmen doubted that the statue would fit through the entrance, but the master had overlooked no considerations. The Asuka Daibutsu proved Tori's thorough knowledge of his craft and his unexcelled artistry, and the Emperor rewarded him with high official rank and a substantial tract of land.

The Asuka Daibutsu survived numerous fires and has been repaired frequently. Most of its tightly-wound, snail-shell curls have been destroyed, and more than half the curls today are clay replicas. Scars under the right eye and the nose mark the relatively undamaged face. One cheek wears "make-up" to hide another mark. Damage from the neck down is so severe that little of the original remains.

Although faithful attempts were made to replicate the original during repairs, adverse economic conditions or drops in Buddhism's popularity made complete restoration impossible. Much make-shift work, therefore, is evident. Still, despite its scars, this venerable Buddha retains substantial grace and beauty from Tori Busshi's original rendition. The plentiful scars and patches relate the proud, 1400-year history of Japan's oldest Shaka image.

III. BUDDHIST IMAGES
– THEIR ATTRIBUTES AND FIGURES –

The Thirty-two Attributes: Certain features of the Asuka Daibutsu – the wisdom protuberance at the crown of the head (*ushnisha*), the three rings of flesh circling the neck, the exceptionally long earlobes, and the light-emitting curl of hair between the eyebrows (*urna*) – are common to all Shaka images. There are thirty-two such features which have remained constant despite the many stylistic variations Buddhist imagery has undergone during its long history. No Buddha or bodhisattva image lacks them. The attributes originated in ancient Indian tradition, which lists them as the signs of a Great Man, signs denoting a superhuman physical condition. Naturally, the living prince Siddartha possessed all thirty-two features. They were thus integral iconographic elements from Buddhist imagery's inception, and today reveal not only identity but certain fundamental religious ideals.

The thirty-two attributes vary slightly in their presentation from one sacred text to another, but the differences are hardly worth note. The *Chido-ron* lists them in the following order.

1. Flatfootedness. The Buddha's feet have no arches.
2. The Imprint of the Wheel. A crest-like, thousand-spoked wheel appears on the soles of Buddha's feet.
3. Finger Length. The Buddha's fingers are exceptionally long and slender.
4. Softness of Hands and Feet. The skin of the Buddha's hands and feet is truly soft and smooth; there is not even the slightest roughness.
5. Webbing. The Buddha has a web-like membrane between his fingers and toes.
6. Special Heel Shape. Both the Buddha's heels are broad, rounded, and perfectly smooth.
7. Instep Height. The Buddha's feet have unusually high insteps.

8. Stag-like Thighs. The flesh of the Buddha's thighs is as supple and firm as a great deer's.
9. Superior Arm Length. The Buddha has exceptionally long arms; when standing, his fingertips reach his knees.
10. Retracted Genitals. The Buddha's genitals are retracted, hidden inside his body.
11. Classically Proportioned Body. The Buddha's body height is equal to his armspread.
12. Blue Body Hair. Blue hairs grow from the pores of the Buddha's skin.
13. Curious Body Hair Growth. All of the Buddha's body hair grows in an upward direction.
14. Golden Skin. The Buddha's whole body gleams with a beautiful golden tone.
15. Halo of Light. The Buddha emits a halo of light which frames his body and extends outward about three meters.
16. Velvet Skin. The Buddha's skin is so smooth and fine-textured that not even the minutest particle of dust will stick to it.
17. Seven Fleshy Regions. The flesh of the Buddha's two feet, palms, shoulders, and the neck is full and abundant.
18. Fleshy Sides. The Buddha's armpits are fleshy, not hollow as with ordinary men.
19. Leonine Body. The Buddha's body has a leonine majesty.
20. Excellent Body Posture. The Buddha always stands firmly and perfectly erect.
21. Shoulder Roundness. Both the Buddha's shoulders are richly covered with flesh.
22. Supernumerary Teeth. The Buddha has forty beautiful, straight teeth.
23. Tooth Arrangement. All the Buddha's teeth are equal in size, and pure white; there are no gaps between the teeth.
24. Large Canine Teeth. The four canine teeth are whiter and sharper than the others.
25. Leonine Cheeks. Both cheeks are full and firm.
26. Flavor-giving Saliva. The Buddha's saliva imparts a delicious taste to everything he eats.

27. Unusual Tongue Length. The Buddha's tongue is thin and flexible; when extended, its tip reaches to the hairline.
28. Vocal Purity. The Buddha's voice is beautifully strong and deep.
29. Deep Blue Eye Color. The pupils of the Buddha's eyes are a clear and beautiful blue, like the sky.
30. Eyelashes. The Buddha has uniquely long, beautiful eyelashes.
31. Urna. The Buddha has a light-emitting, clockwise curl of white hair growing between his eyebrows.
32. Ushnisha. The Buddha has a protuberance of wisdom, shaped somewhat like a topknot, on the crown of his head.

Besides the thirty-two attributes, there are also eighty secondary characteristics. Essentially a more detailed presentation of the thirty-two attributes, the secondary characteristics are quite complex. The two sets of identifying properties together almost completely describe a Buddha.

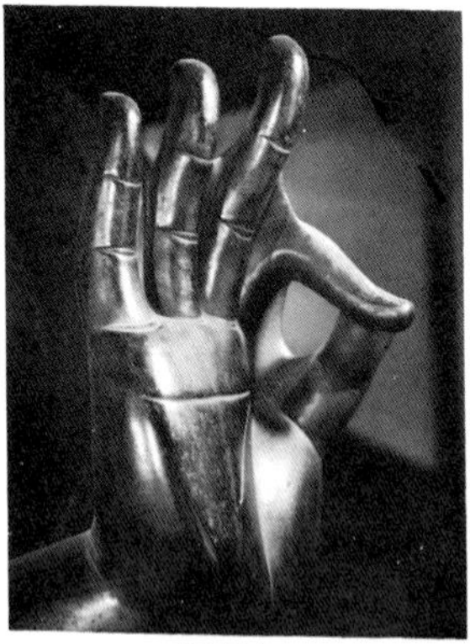

Webbing

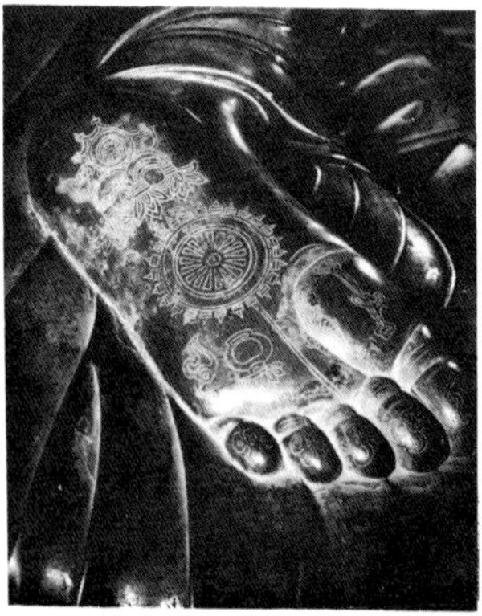

The Imprint of the Wheel

Mudra – the Speaking Hands: While the thirty-two attributes and the eighty secondary characteristics help us distinguish between a Buddha and a bodhisattva, they do not permit us to tell Shaka from Yakushi, Amida, or even Miroku. How then to identify a particular Buddha or bodhisattva?

A particularly effective identification method is hand positions, or *mudra*. The reader certainly will agree that the hands or fingers can be as expressive as words. A finger raised to one's lips to hush someone is an example. A more complicated example is the signs a catcher or the base coaches use in baseball. In Japan, a raised little finger refers to one's wife or sweetheart, while the thumb refers to one's father. The hand positions utilized in Buddhist imagery is similarly expressive. Each Buddha and bodhisattva has typical *mudra* which identify the image and either point up an important characteristic or indicate the deity's function in the Buddhist pantheon.

The hand positions to learn first are those relating to the Nyorai, the Buddhas. Three positions common to all Buddhas are the Mudra of the Turning of the Wheel of the Law, the Mudra of Giving, and the "Do Not Fear" Mudra. Other examples are the Mudra of Touching the Ground, indicating a Shaka Nyorai, and the Mudra of the Knowledge Fist and the Concentration Mudra of the Dharma World, denoting Dainichi Nyorai. The Mudra of the Amida of the Nine Classes is a group of nine positions using both hands. They indicate nine states, from Lower Class, Lower Life, to Upper Class, Upper Life. Forms of the Mudra of Appeasement represent the six lower and middle states; meditating poses represent the three states in the Upper Class. The accompanying sketch shows these and other hand positions.

Over the centuries, the number of figures in the Buddhist pantheon increased tremendously. Esoteric Buddhism in particular tended to include borrowed heathen deities in their imagery. As these imports rose to important positions in Buddhist tradition, they acquired identifying iconography appropriate for their stations. This proliferation naturally affected the system of *mudra*. The artistic expression of a few

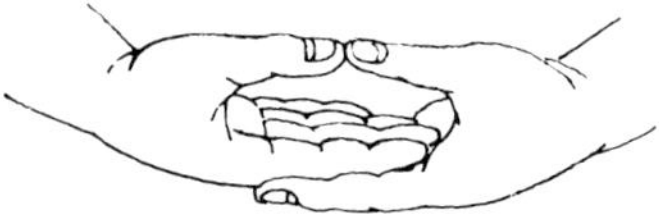

Dharma World of Concentration

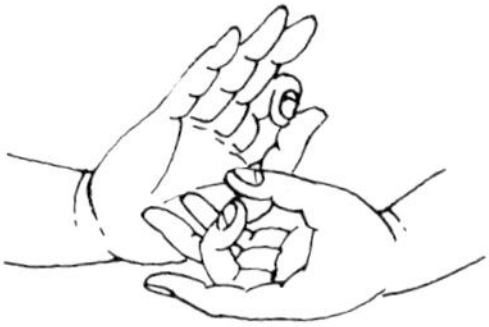

Turning Wheel of Law

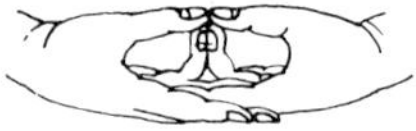

Lower Class, Upper Life

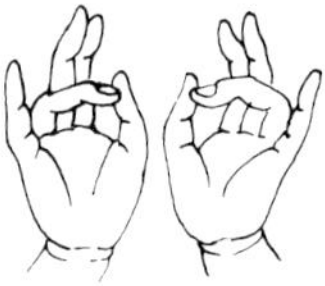

Lower Class, Middle Life

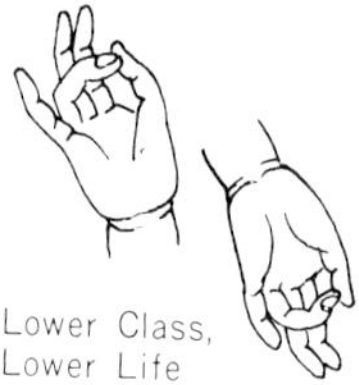

Lower Class, Lower Life

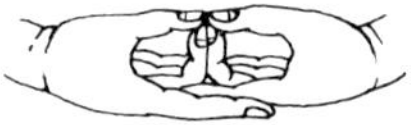

Middle Class, Upper Life

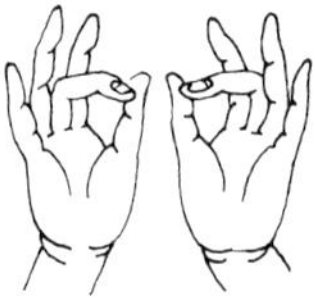

Middle Class, Middle Life

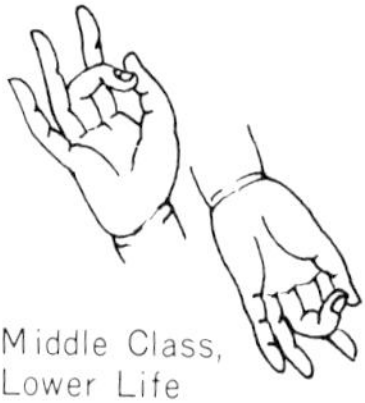

Middle Class, Lower Life

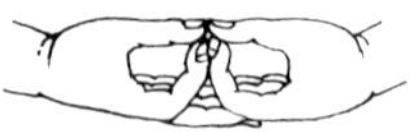

Upper Class, Upper Life

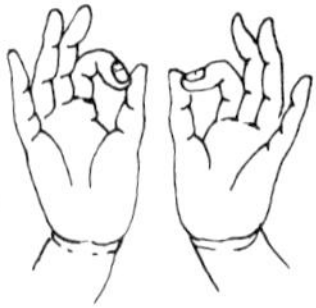

Upper Class, Middle Life

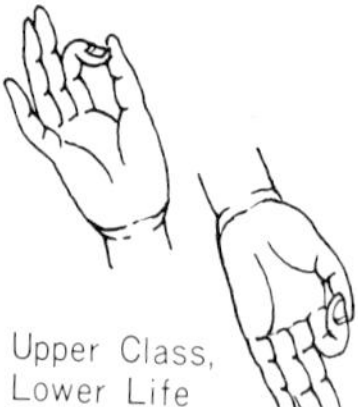

Upper Class, Lower Life

clearly distinct religious figures had been simple and direct. More and subtler signs were needed to express adequately the growing complexity and richness of Japanese Buddhism.

Even after a person recognizes *mudra* he will still experience difficulty identifying some images. Both Shaka and Yakushi, for example, have the same thirty-two attributes, eighty secondary characteristics and *mudra*. How, then, can the viewer be certain? For pre-Nara Period images, written records must be examined, which causes occasional disagreement among scholars as to whether a particular statue is Shaka, Yakushi, or perhaps Amida. To help with identification, images came to carry implements. Yakushi, the Healer, carries in his left hand a covered apothecary's jar. The jar is an unmistakable sign, just as today the doctor's black bag clearly marks his profession. This method of identification – providing an image with a utensil to indicate its character or function – is precise and convenient.

Some implements carried by images are sutra scrolls, medicine jars, fly whisks (symbolizing obedience to the law against harming any living thing), jewels, sistra, and rosaries. Esoteric Buddhism's favorite implements are single-, three-, and five-pronged *vajra* (a thunderbolt symbol), *vajra* bells, jeweled reliquaries, sacred swords, ropes (symbolizing the snare of love by which Buddha catches and holds Sentient Beings to his teachings), and the lotus.

Despite precise classification, the great number of images still causes confusion. Yakushi with his medicine jar, Jizo Bosatsu with a metal rattle, Kannon with the lotus, and Nio (the Two Deva Kings) with their *vajra* are all simple enough. But others are not so simple: the six-armed Nyoirin Kannon, the eight-armed Fukukenjaku Kannon, and especially the Thousand-Armed Kannon hold a variety of objects in their many hands.

Poses and Minor Accounterments: Except for the reclining Parinirvana Buddha, Buddhist images fall into two major poses; those standing, and those seated.

Many images in the former group stand stiffly erect facing

front. Both legs are straight, and both feet planted firmly on the ground pointing forward. Examples of standing images are the Shaka Nyorai (photo 6) of Saidai-ji Temple, Todai-ji Temple's Amida Nyorai (photo 9), Jingo-ji's Yakushi Nyorai (photo 21), Genko-ji's Yakushi Nyorai (photo 22), Horyu-ji's Guze Kannon (photo 33), Kudara Kannon (photo 45), and Yumetagai Kannon (photo 47) and Yakushi-ji's Sho Kannon (photo 32). The Eleven-Headed Kannon (photo 37) of Hokke-ji Temple displays a more relaxed frontal pose by placing one foot slightly forward on its pedestal. This stance distributes the body weight unevenly and results in softer, curved body lines. The vigorous Kicking Stance, with one leg poised as if to stamp down in rage, is common to the Shi Tenno and other guardian figures. Good examples are images (photo 84) in the Kaidan-in of Todai-ji. The Amida Descending from the Clouds (Raigo Amida), in the fresco of Byodo-in's Phoenix Hall, typifies the lovely, free-moving Dancing Pose.

The most common sitting position is the full-lotus, with both legs crossed. The Amida Nyorai images in Byodo-in (photo 12) and Hokai-ji (photo 13) Temples are good examples. The feet rest on the knees, soles facing up. The lotus pose variations are the position of good fortune, with the right leg around the left and on top, and the demon-subduing pose, with the left leg on top.

Other figures sit in chairs and plant both feet firmly on their pedestal. The half-lotus position is a variation of this, with one leg down and the other crossed over it, foot resting in the lap. Almost all Miroku Bosatsu images take this pensive position. Two examples are in Horyu-ji and Chugu-ji (photos 28, 29) Temples. The Nyoirin Kannon images in Muro-ji and Kanshin-ji (photos 49, 50) Temples adopt the royal ease position. One frequently finds the Raigo Amida Triad in a kneeling position with both heels raised off the floor. Bon Ten in To-ji Temple sits in a relaxed cross-legged position.

There are no fixed rules governing the position a particular image takes, although the full-lotus pose is perhaps most commonly associated with Buddha images. Bodhisattva often stand erect, except for Miroku, who usually sits contemplating ways to save man. Myoo and other guardian figures often stand in the Kicking Stance.

Buddhist images stand or sit upon various pedestals. The most frequently used is the Lotus Throne, traditionally an eightypetalled lotus blossom – although one occasionally encounters a thousand-petalled lotus. Originally a quite simple design, the Lotus Throne underwent changes over the centuries until it became quite intricate and complex.

The World Mountain Throne symbolizes the World Mountain of Hindu tradition, which was introduced into Buddhism as a dwelling place for the gods. The Shaka Triad (photo 4) in Horyu-ji's Main Hall, and the Yakushi images (photos 16, 19) in Yakushi-ji and Horin-ji Temples sit on World Mountain Thrones. The robes worn by these images drape slightly over the pedestal edges to provide a decorative effect. This is called the Draped Throne. Koryu-ji's Miroku Bosatsu (photo 29) sits in a meditative half-lotus on a Lotus Throne overlaid by the Draped Throne.

Other pedestals in use are the Rock Throne: the Wave Throne, resembling waves beating upon the beach; the Cloud Throne; the lotus throne of upturned lotus leaves; animal thrones of elephants, lions, peacocks, and other birds and beasts; and Shoryo pedestals shaped like devils or heavenly beings upon which the deities stand. Certain pedestals are associated with particular images. The World Mountain Throne belongs solely to Buddha images, while the Lotus Throne supports either Buddhas or bodhisattva. The Cloud Throne appears with Raigo Amida. Devils, heavenly beings, or the Rock Throne hold the Five Great Myoo, the Shi Tenno, and other guardian figures.

The halos behind Buddhist images symbolize and stylize the light emitted from the Buddha in the 15th and 31st of the thirty-two attributes, and can be considered an integral part of the image. Halos exist in a variety of shapes. One finds round halos, pointed-oval halos, spoked halos, jewel-shaped halos, body halos, and a double-circle full halo. Halos are also classified by design and detail into Thousand-Buddha halos, arabesque halos, cloud halos, flame halos, halos of ropes of flame, and others. Amida Nyorai usually has a pointed-oval halo, as do the Amida images in Byodo-in and Hokai-ji (photos 12, 13). The Rushana Buddhas in Toshodai-ji and Todai-ji both have Thousand-Buddha halos. Flame halos usually accompany Myoo and guardian figures.

The clothing and body ornaments Buddhist images wear derive from clothing worn in India during Prince Siddartha's lifetime. The camlet he wore after attaining enlightenment set the style for Buddha images. The bodhisattva's dress developed from pre-enlightenment styles. Both styles thus originated from clothing favored by the Indian nobility of Buddha's time.

Shakamuni walked barefooted from his father's palace wearing a single piece of cloth and no ornaments of any kind. The cloth he wore was a priest's coarse robe. Buddha images today wear the robe two ways. The *hendan uken* leaves the right shoulder and arm bare. The *tsuken* has both shoulders and both arms covered. All images of Buddha but one are dressed in like fashion. The exception is Dainichi Nyorai of esoteric Buddhism, who dresses in bodhisattva style. Bodhisattva garb, styled from Gautama's clothing before he left his princely life, is more elaborate than the Buddha cloth. Furthermore, bodhisattva tie their hair into topknots, and wear gorgeous crowns, ear ornaments, necklaces, bracelets, brooches, and other accessories. Sometimes they even wear footwear.

Although Myoo also take their dress style from Guatama's pre-Enlightenment life, they are far less refined and elegant than bodhisattva. One might call their dress crudely masculine. They may decorate themselves with skull necklaces, and snake or tiger skin. Heavenly beings may be men, women, or personified birds and animals. Their clothing varies accordingly. Male figures like the Shi Tenno wear armor, helmets, and leggings, giving them an unmistakable military appearance. Female figures wear colorful clothing and a full complement of ornaments, from shoes to necklaces and crowns.

IV. MATERIALS AND TECHNIQUES

Some people consider too analytical and materialistic the inquiry into materials and techniques used to produce Buddhist images. They say the inquiry is unrelated to religious beliefs and the religious spirit. The counterargument, of course, is that the deeper one's background awareness, the better appreciation one will have of the spirit of the age an image dates from, and of the emotions the artist invested in his work. To classify and otherwise study materials or sculpting methods used to produce Buddhist images, at any rate, is certainly not without some significance.

The five primary materials used for Buddhist images in Japan are wood, bronze, dry lacquer, stucco, and stone. Materials like silver, iron, and paper were also used, but the statues made of those materials comprise an insignificant percent of the total number.

Wood: In stories relating to Kannon worship, one frequently reads of images made of *reiboku*, literally "spirit" or "deceased soul" wood. Buddhist images sculpted of the "aromatic wood that was floated down the Naniwa Tsu," and those of the wood with the "gold-like brilliance" are *reiboku* images. What the *reiboku* stories are saying is that ordinary wood was not used for sculpting Buddhist images. Wood was selected only after careful scrutiny. To meet Buddhism's needs and requirements, the preferred wood would have to be fragrant, beautifully finished, easy to work with, and readily available in large quantity. Japanese cypress best met these requirements, and is the material used in the great majority of wooden Buddhist images in Japan. The layman should note, too, that while stone and rock images outnumber others in India and China, wood images predominate in Japan.

Regarding wooden images, the story can be told of the time a few years ago a heartless university student broke a finger off the right hand of Koryu-ji Temple's famous Miroku Bosatsu statue. At the time, a respected art historian, whose special discipline was sculpture, was asked what wood the statue was made of. His reply was Japanese cypress. Actually, the Miroku statue is made of red pine. My point in relating the incident, however, is not to stress the art historian's mistake, but to point out that his answer suggests the preponderen use of cypress when wood is the sculpting material.

As a general rule, with the exception being images that use a special sandalwood, Buddhist images made of wood other than cypress are either pre-Nara Period works or second-rate productions located in the provinces. The Kudara (Paekche) Kannon (photo 45) in Horyu-ji Temple, and the Miroku Bosatsu image (photo 28) in Chugu-ji Temple are made of camphor wood, but almost uniformly the most representative Nara Period sculptures – such as those in Toshodai-ji and Daian-ji Temples – are cypress. Cypress is predominent even after the Heian Period. Other woods used are cherry, zelkova, and pine. On rare occasions one may find an image made of paulowania.

The two general categories of wood sculptures are unfinished images and those of wood finished with color or lacquer. Works done in unfinished wood are the Seiryoji-style Shaka Nyorai (photo 6) in Saidai-ji Temple, the Yakushi Nyorai images in Shin Yakushi-ji (photo 20) and Akishino-dera (photo 18) Temples, the Miroku Butsu (photo 31) in Todai-ji Temple, and the Yakushi Nyorai images in Genko-ji (photo 22) and Jingo-ji Temples (photo 21). Other than slight touches of *sumi* or vermilion color on the eyes or mouth, all these images rely completely on the natural beauty of unfinished wood. The wood grain is used to maximum effect throughout.

The Juichimen Kannon (photo 37) of Hokke-ji Temple and the Kumen Kannon (photo 34) of Horyu-ji Temple (said to be carried from T'ang China) are of unfinished sandalwood. Sandalwood's chief value is its fragrance, and a finish naturally would detract from or totally neutralize its olfactory function.

The most common wood finishes are gilded lacquer and paint. The lacquer used for gilding is Japanese rhus lacquer applied with special techniques. After lacquering an image, gold leaf is applied. The resultant lustre resembles the gold plate finish on metal statues, and faithfully fulfils the Buddha attribute that demands a beautiful golden tone. A great many wooden images in Japan are finished this way. The oldest among them is the Guze Kannon (photo 33) of esoteric Buddhism located in Yumedono Hall of Horyu-ji Temple. Other memorable works with a gilded lacquer finish are the four Nara Period images (photo 10) in Saidai-ji Temple's Pagoda, and the Heian Period Amida Nyorai images in Phoenix Hall of Byodo-in (photo 12) and Joruri-ji (photo 11) Temples.

Painted images include the Juichimen Kannon (photo 39) in Muro-ji Temple, in which even the halo is painted beautifully, Kissho Ten (photo 101) of Joruri-ji Temple, Nyoirin Kannon (photo 50) of Kanshin-ji Temple, and the Godai Kokuzo images (photo 71) in Jingo-ji Temple.

Wooden images are classfied by sculpting method into two groups. They either derive from a single piece of wood (*ichibokucho*), or are assembled from separately carved sections (*yosegizukuri*). In the former method, the hands and feet – up to the wrists or ankles – may be attached separately, and occasionally the pedestal will be sculpted from the same piece of wood. The Kudara (Paekche) Kannon (photo 45) of Horyu-ji, the Miroku Bosatsu (photo 28) of Chugu-ji, and the Miroku Bosatsu (photo 29) of Koryu-ji Temples are Asuka Period productions carved from single-pieces of wood. Some discontinuity occurs between these single-piece images and *ichiboku* works dating from late Nara (late eighth century) to early Heian (middle of ninth century).

Ichibokucho images like the late Nara Period Yakushi Nyorai and Taho Nyorai of Toshodai-ji Temple, and Daian-ji Temple's Yoryu Kannon (photo 54), Bato Kannon (photo 55), and the Shi Tenno probably developed directly from the wooden form used under dry lacquer images that were popular in middle-Nara. In other words, the wooden form formerly used with dry lacquer images shed its covering and developed as an independent type of *ichibokucho*. Carving techniques in these late Nara Period images developed to produce early Heian Period images like the Juichimen Kannon of Hokke-ji Temple and the Yakushi Nyorai images in Genko-ji and Jingo-ji Temples.

Yosegizukuri, the second wood sculpting category, is a highly rational technique that originated in the late Heian Period. If an image must be sculpted from a single piece of wood, obvious difficulties present themselves. Transportation, of course, was troublesome when heavy wood was used, or when an image was large. Furthermore, when a single piece of wood dried it split easily along the grain, occasionally being cleft completely into two or three pieces. To offset the shortcomings of using a single piece of wood, a method was first introduced where statues were carved hollow, and a cover placed over the hollowing hole when the statue was completed. This was not completely satisfactory, however, and to solve all problems an entirely new sculpting method, the *yosegi* method, was introduced. In this method, an image's various parts were sculpted separately and joined together to form the whole. The *yosegi* method meant, first of all, no restrictions regarding size. Thus, large images could be produced with little trouble. Jocho (? – 1057) perfected the *yosegi* method in middle Heian. The Amida Nyorai images in Byodo-in (photo 12) and Hokai-ji (photo 13) Temples are both noteworthy works by him. Unkei (early thirteenth century) also mastered the *yosegi* method. He and his disciples produced the Nio (photos 92, 95) masterpieces guarding Nandaimon Gate of Todai-ji Temple. These two giants stand thirty-feet in height.

Bronze: The Asuka Daibutsu mentioned earlier is the oldest bronze Buddha in Japan, and the Nara Daibutsu – Rushana Butsu (photo 23) of Todai-ji Temple – is the largest. The entire country's resources were mobilized over a number of years to produce the Rushana image. It was cast in seven stages, from bottom to top. Other representative bronze images are the Shaka Triad (photo 4) in Kondo Hall of Horyu-ji Temple, produced by Tori Busshi; Horyu-ji Temple's Amida

Triad (photo 8); the Yakushi Nyorai head in Kofuku-ji Temple's National Treasure Hall (photo 17); Yumetagai Kannon in Horyu-ji Temple (photo 47); and Yakushi-ji Temple's Yakushi Nyorai, Nikko and Gakko (photos 17, 61, 62), and Sho Kannon (photo 32).

Various methods were used to produce bronze images. The rough form might be mud, or wax covered with clay. Boiling bronze poured into the latter melted the wax and allowed the image to adopt the outlines of the clay. Another method was to place bronze sheets on the basic mold and to pound them into form, the so-called *oshidashi* method. Examples of Nara Period images effected using the *oshidashi* method are in Horyu-ji and Toshodai-ji Temples.

Buddhist images made of silver, iron, or other metals are also extant. The tiny silver Amida Nyorai on the crown of Fuku-Kenjyaku Kannon (photo 42) in Todai-ji Temple's Sangatsudo Hall is especially famous. Kofuku-ji Temple houses an interesting silver hand, all that remains of an image probably destroyed by fire. Judging from the size of the land, the image probably was larger than life-size. If in existence it certainly would be rare and valuable.

Iron casting techniques are more difficult than bronze, and perhaps that is why few iron images remain. From the Kamakura Period on, iron images were cast in various spots throughout the country but they were mostly quite small. Furthermore, as a material for forming fine extremities like fingers, ears, and so forth, bronze is superior to iron.

Stucco: A wooden frame is constructed first of all, with wire used to form fingers and other fine details. Straw or flax is wrapped around the wooden and wire frame, and plastered first with rough and then fine mud. The surface is finished with extremely fine mud combined with a mica/clod mixture. Some images are then painted with color. This method came to Japan in the Hakuho and Nara Periods directly from T'ang China, where it enjoyed great popularity. Very few later period stucco images exist in Japan. Important and well-known stucco images are: Nyoirin Kannon of Oka-dera Temple, Miroku Butsu (photo 27) of Taima-ji Temple, the Paranirvana Shaka (photo 7) in Horyu-ji's Five-storied Pagoda, Horyu-ji's Monju, Bon Ten, Taishaku Ten, Shi Tenno, and the Nio (photo 93) of Chumon Gate. Also, the Nikko, Gakko (photos 64, 65), Shukongoshin (photo 96), Kissho Ten (photo 101), and Benzai Ten (photo 102) images in Todai-ji's Sangatsudo Hall and the Shi Tenno (photos 80, 84) in the same temple's Kaidanin, and Shinyakushi-ji Temple's Main Hall images of Basara (photo 98) and the other Juni Jinsho (photo 99).

Benzai Ten in Sangatsudo Hall sorely needs repair. In its present condition, however, together with the Kissho Ten image in the same hall, it clearly reveals how it was created. In the Bon Ten and Taishaku Ten images in Horyu-ji Temple one is pleasantly surprised to view under damaged shoes feet carved precisely with five toes. One is glimpsing artistic devotion and attention to detail.

Dry lacquer: Dry lacquer images, like stucco images, were produced mainly during the Nara Period. Almost no examples exist from later dates.

One method of construction, much like stucco images, is first to give these images their general shape in clay. Lacquer and flax are applied in turn to the clay and the fine parts of the image formed. When the many layers of lacquer and flax harden sufficiently the clay is removed from the inside to leave the outer papier-mache shell.

A second method is to construct the basic figure of wood, and to apply the layers of lacquer and flax directly to the wood. The wooden core is left inside the image. This wooden-core was sculpted with greater and greater care until it eventually became an independent style of *ichiboku* sculpture. When viewing a dry lacquer image one never knows for certain what great labors might have been put into sculpting its wooden core.

The oldest extant dry lacquer images in Japan are the Shi Tenno (photo 83) of Taima-ji Temple's Kondo Hall, thought to date from the Emperor Tenmu's reign (673 – 686). Beards give these images striking reality, and the general lack of movement provides them with age. One of the best-known dry lacquer statues is the triple-faced, six-armed Ashura (photo 97) in Kofuku-ji Temple. The secrets of its popularity may be the expressions on its three faces and the wonderful lines formed by the slender arms. Ashura is one of the eight Hachi Bushu. The Hachi Bushu and Ten Great Disciple images in Kofuku-ji Temple represent the finest in Nara Period dry lacquer sculpture.

Sangatsudo Hall of Todai-ji Temple ranks with Kofuku-ji Temple for displaying masterful dry lacquer images. Taken as a group, moreover, the Sangatsudo Hall images have no peers. The group includes the central Fuku Kenjyaku Kannon image (photo 42), Bon Ten (photo 88), Taishaku Ten, Kongo Rikishi (photo 88), and Shi Tenno (photo 85). Toshodai-ji Temple displays numerous wooden-core dry lacquer images. The central Rushana Butsu image (photo 25), the Senju Kannon (photo 52), and the Yakushi Nyorai are all giants among Japan's dry lacquer images. The Juichimen Kannon images in Shorin-ji Temple (photo 36) and Kannon-ji Temple (photo 38) are also beautiful examples of wooden-core dry lacquer sculptures. Most dry lacquer images are found in Nara and Yamato. Mention must also be made of the Senju Kannon (photo 51) in Osaka's Fujii-dera Temple, ranked on a par with Toshodai-ji Temple's masterful Senju Kannon. The early Nara Period Amida Triad in Horyu-ji's Denpodo Hall are wooden-core dry lacquer images that are very close to *ichiboku* sculptures.

Stone: As mentioned earlier, stone was the chief material used for sculpting Buddhist images in China and India, while Japanese sculptors primarily used wood and bronze. Japan's first stupas also were wooden. When a stone image appears in Japan, the temptation is to imagine special circumstances that prohibited using other materials. The primary reason stone was not used is that Japan lacked an appropriate stone material.

China and India are blessed with stone materials.

Stone images that immediately come to mind are the splendid Hakuho Period Triad in Ishii-dera Temple of Sakurai City, and the famous group of thirteen Nara Period stone images in Zuto, Nara City. Famous groupings of stone buddhas are found in the eastern suburbs of Nara City, in Oya-dera Temple in Utsunomiya City in Tochigi Prefecture, and in Usuki City in Kyushu.

The largest stone images in Japan are the engraved Miroku Butsu image in Ono-dera Temple on the way to Muro in Nara City, and a similar Miroku Butsu located on Kasaoki Mountain. Nara's Jurin-in Temple boasts of a rare group of stone Buddhas in which Jizo Bosatsu (photo 67) is the central deity. Other figures in the group include the Juo, Taishaku Ten, Shaka, Fudo Myoo, and others. The entire group is in a ten-foot-wide, ten-foot-deep cave-like niche. The setting is like a miniature of the cave-temples found on the Asian mainland.

Most stone images, unlike sculptures done in other materials, are exposed to weathering. They usually were built or commissioned by commoners, while aristocrats left memorials to their own or their families' names by ordering wood or perhaps gold images, or even commissioning entire temples. Often one will come upon a stone Jizo Bosatsu image standing at the outskirts of a town or village to ward off evil and sickness. Jizo is very close to the Japanese common people, and most stone Jizo images located at the foot of mountains, or alongside roads, are associated with some folklore of the region, and relate to local religious beliefs.

V. BUDDHIST IMAGES: SHAPE AND *KOKORO*

Shaka Nyorai: The Tanjo Shaka depicts Shaka at birth. He emerged from his mother's right armpit, immediately stood up, and walked seven steps. He gestured to heaven and then to earth, and said, "All in Heaven and all on Earth I rule."

Shaka's birthday celebration is April 8th, and Tanjo Shaka is the principal image worshipped on that day. The newborn Shaka possessed the thirty-two attributes, and the Tanjo Shaka image – tiny though it is – displays all thirty-two attributes. Generally, Tanjo Shaka images are between five and fifteen centimeters in height. The Todai-ji Temple Tanjo Shaka (photo 1), at 46.9 centimeters, is quite large. It is displayed during *Kanbutsu* services (held on anniversary of Buddha's birth; water or hydrangea tea is poured on Shaka image) before the temple's Daibutsu Hall. Most Tanjo Shaka hold their right hand up, although occasionally one finds a statue with its left hand raised. The left hand raised is either the artisan's preference or an inheritance from similar sculptures found in southern China.

Shaka left his father's palace at twenty-nine to begin six years of trials and agonies searching for the path of truth. The gaunt figures of Shaka undergoing religious austerities and Shaka descending from the mountain are favorite themes in zen paintings. Extremely few images using those two themes exist in Japan. Another well-known theme is the scene where Shaka overcomes varous evils and temptations and attains enlightenment beneath the Bodhi tree. In that scene his left hand rests on one knee and his right hand is lowered to let his fingers touch the ground.

After attaining enlightenment, Buddha wandered some two hundred miles to Sarnath, near Benares, and preached his first sermon. From that day to his death Buddha visited all parts of

India and gradually gained many disciples. He proclaimed his message to all and helped sincere inquirers master the promise and power he preached. It is the teaching, proselytizing figure of Shaka that we find most frequently in Japan. The right hand forms the "Do Not Fear" Mudra, while the left forms the Mudra of Giving. Occasionally both hands form the Mudra of the Turning of the Wheel of Law. The Asuka Daibutsu (photo 2) is the teaching, proselytizing Shaka, as are the Shaka Nyorai (photo 4) in Kondo Hall of Horyu-ji Temple, and the Shaka Nyorai images (photos 3, 5) in Muro-ji and Kaniman-ji Temples.

Shaka entered nirvana at the age of eighty. The paranirvana image shows Buddha surrounded by disciples, and many birds and beasts. Buddha lies on his right side, facing west, with his head on a pillow to the north. The Shaka Nehan (photo 7) in the Pagoda of Horyu-ji Temple is the oldest extant paranirvana image in Japan.

The Seiryoji-style Shaka is an image of the living Shaka that fits into a special category. A Japanese priest named Chonen visited Sung China and supposedly brought back this image, sculpted in copy of a Sung image. It was further copied in Japan at Saidai-ji (photo 9), Toshodai-ji, and other temples.

Amida Nyorai: According to Buddhist teachings, Amida of the Pure Land will save all men. The seated Amida Nyorai (photo 8) in Horyu-ji's Hozoden Treasury is a bronze image of the Hakuho Period. It depicts three lotus stems shooting up from a pond. Lotus flower pedestals on the stems seat Amida in the center, and the bodhisattva attendants Kannon and Seishi on either side. A screen in back is decorated with lotus leaf designs and reliefs of heavenly beings. Amida Nyorai's hands form the "Do Not Fear" Mudra and the Mudra of Giving. Other Amida images frequently show the Mudra of the Turning of the Wheel of Law.

From the Fujiwara to the Kamakura Periods, many Amida images show *hendan uken* style clothing like the images in Byodo-in Temple (photo 12) and Hokai-ji Temple (photo 13).

Also, with the spread of Pure Land Buddhism, groups of nine Amida Nyorai images (photo 11) – one to receive souls into each of nine classes of nirvana – were produced in large numbers. As mentioned in detail earlier, the nine classes were from Lower Class, Lower Life, to Upper Class, Upper Life. A soul's particular class and life depended on the depth of spiritual commitment and attainment the soul achieved. Upper Life (combined with Upper, Middle, and Lower Classes) uses the Meditation Mudra; Middle Life (combined with Upper, Middle, and Lower Classes) uses the Preaching Mudra; and Lower Life (combined with Upper, Middle, and Lower Classes) uses the Raigo (coming down of Amida to greet the soul) Mudra. Each Life/Class combination has slight variations on the same mudra.

Yakushi Nyorai: One of man's greatest afflictions is disease and sickness. All glory and wordly possessions seem empty indeed when man lies gravely ill. Fervent prayers by the sick for recovery are the same today as in ancient days. One difference, however, is that people in our present age, an age which has witnessed considerable advances in medical practices and medicines, probably cannot truly imagine the poignant ring of prayers the ancients raised to ask the Gods and Buddhas for help. The Buddha who cures physical illness and dispels spiritual confusion, Yakushi Nyorai, came to Japan not long after Buddhism's arrival. Yakushi devotion fast spread throughout all segments of Japanese society. At the highest levels, the Imperial family and the aristocracy prayed to him. At the lower levels, commoners turned to the "Physician of Souls" for help.

Emperor Tenmu (reigned 673 – 686) ordered Yakushi-ji Temple's construction mainly because the Empress was sick. Although the Empress recovered, whether through Yakushi Nyorai's intercession or not, the Emperor died before construction was completed. The Empress became ruler and saw the temple through to completion in 697. The temple originally was located in Asuka, but was removed to Nara in

718 when the Capital was reconstructed there. Although scholarly opinion varies on whether the central Yakushi image (photo 16) in Yakushi-ji Temple is a Hakuho Period production carried to Nara, or was executed after the temple was reconstructed in Nara, there is general agreement on the image's high artistic and historical value. The wooden Yakushi Nyorai image in Horin-ji predates the Yakushi-ji Temple image, and reveals the Asuka Period style. The central Yakushi image of the old Yamada-dera Temple, of which only the head remains, is seen today in Kofuku-ji Temple's Kondo Hall (photo 17) and is a representative Hakuho Period work. A number of imposing Yakushi images appear in the Heian Period. Representative are the seated images in Akishino-dera (photo 18) and Shin Yakushi-ji Temples, and the standing images in Jingo-ji (photo 21) and Genko-ji (photo 22) Temples.

Like other Buddhas, most Yakushi images display the "Do Not Fear" Mudra and the Mudra of Giving. Heian Period and later Yakushi images usually hold an apothecary's jar in the left hand.

Dainichi Nyorai: Dainichi, also called Rushana Butsu or Daibi Rushana Nyorai, is the basic, unified Nyorai. The finest expressions of Dainichi's spirit are the Daibutsu (photo 23) of Todai-ji Temple and the central image in Toshodai-ji Temple (photo 25). The Todai-ji Daibutsu sits on a thousand-leaved lotus, each leaf of which represents one world. Shaka appears in each world to preach the Buddhist law. Each Shaka in each world also sits on a thousand-leaved lotus, each leaf representing a world in which he appears as a bodhisattva. Rushana Butsu, therefore, sits above 1,000 x 1,000 x 1,000, or 10 billion worlds. The Toshodai-ji Temple Rushana Butsu has a thousand-Buddha halo. The tiny images express one thousand incarnations of Shaka.

Enjo-ji Temple's Dainichi Nyorai (photo 24) was effected by the young Unkei. The image represents Dainichi as a bodhisattva preaching in the Kongo World, and his hands form the Mudra of the Fighting Fist.

Shokannon: When Kannon is referred to merely as Kannon Bosatsu, the reference is to Shokannon. Images with special names like the Kudara Kannon (photo 45), the Yumetagai Kannon (photo 47), and the Guze Kannon (photo 33) are all Shokannon images. Originally, Shokannon stood with Seishi Bosatsu as an attendant at the side of Amida Nyorai. Later he appeared alone as the principle image in a temple, such as Guze Kannon mentioned above and Shokannon (photo 32) in Yakushi-ji Temple. Shokannon frequently wears a crown topped with tiny Amida images.

Juichimen Kannon: Eleven-faced Kannon images first appeared in the Nara Period, well before esoteric Buddhism's advent. Shorin-ji Temple's Juichimen Kannon (photo 36) formerly was in Jingu-ji Temple. Together with Kannon-ji Temple's Juichimen Kannon (Photo 38), it is an important Nara Period work. Tradition holds that the Juichimen Kannon (photo 37) in Hokke-ji Temple was produced by the Indian monk Tenjiku in the Heian Period with the Empress Komei (701 – 760) in mind. The Kumen (nine-faced) Kannon (photo 34) is basically the eleven-faced Kannon minus two faces. The eleven-faced Kannon (photo 39) in Muro-ji Temple, finished in color, boasts of particularly beautiful patterns in its halo.

Fuku Kenjaku Kannon: *Kenjaku* refers to the rope and snare this Kannon uses to snare and hold fast humans who refuse salvation and act like wild beasts or fish floundering about in the sea. The *fuku* stresses that while beasts will sometimes escape from traps, and fish from nets, Kannon's snares and ropes permit no men to escape salvation. Japanese reverence for Fuku Kenjaku Kannon, like that for Juichimen Kannon, began soon after Buddhism came to Japan. Images appear beginning in the Nara Period. The most representative Fuku Kenjaku Kannon image (photo 42) is in Sangatsudo Hall of Todai-ji Temple. Images dating from the Nara Period are in Daian-ji (photo 44) and Koryu-ji Temples. The Fuku Kenjyaku Kannon (photo 43) in Kofuku-ji Temple is an outstanding work restored in the Kamakura Period by Kokei, the great sculptor Unkei's father.

Senju Kannon: This Kannon has one thousand hands and one thousand eyes with which to save mankind. Like Juichimen and Fuku Kenjaku Kannon, Senju Kannon has been reverred by Japanese since Buddhism's arrival in Japan. The images in Toshodai-ji (photo 52) and Fujii-dera (photo 51) Temples are masterpieces of the Nara Period. Both have exactly one-thousand hands. Later Senju Kannons have only twenty hands on either side (the central two hands are not counted) but are thousand-handed Kannons because each hand saves twenty-five worlds. Counting the central hands, the total number of actual arms and hands on such images is forty-two.

Roku Kannon: Tendai Buddhism referred to Shokannon, Juichimen, Senju, Fuku Kenjaku, Bato, and Nyoirin Kannons as the Roku (Six) Kannon. In Shingon (True Word) Buddhism, Fuku Kenjaku was replaced by Juntei. Sometimes Fuku Kenjaku and Juntei are included together, and the group of Kannons is called Shichi (Seven) Kannon.

Miroku: While Kannon, Fugen and others are imaginary figures existing only in doctrine, Miroku actually served as a disciple of Shaka. He dwells at present in Tusita, in the Inner Temple of the Palace of Seven Jewels. There he practices austerities and contemplates ways to save man. He will return to Earth 56 billion 70 million years after Buddha's death, and after attaining enlightenment himself will lead man to salvation. Two general types of Miroku statues thus exist. One type is Miroku after enlightenment, as represented by the images in Kondo Hall (photo 27) of Taima-ji and Hokuendo Hall (photo 30) of Kofuku-ji Temples. The other type is Miroku in Tusita contemplating ways to save mankind. That image is seen in Chugu-ji (photo 28) and Koryu-ji (photo 29) Temples. Taima-ji Temple's Miroku Butsu (photo 27) is a magnificant stucco image of the Hakuho Period. Kofuku-ji Temple's

Miroku Butsu (photo 30) is a typical Kamakura sculpture effected by Unkei and his disciples Genkei and Seikei. The image sits solidly on an eight-cornered Draped Throne. The Chugu-ji and Koryu-ji Temple Miroku Bosatsu images are world famous, and are referred to in every treatise on early Japanese sculpture.

Monju and Fugen: Monju, together with Kannon, is reverred widely in Japan. He was born in India shortly after Shaka's death and was in frequent contact with Buddha's ten great disciples. He was a man of superior intelligence who played a major role in editing Buddhist scriptures. Stories in Buddhist sutras tell of Monju visiting Yuima (Vimalakirti) and arguing about the Buddhist priesthood, and of his travelling far southward and dispatching Zenzai Doji still further south to spread Buddha's word. Monju's spirit is said to rest in China's Mt. Godai (Wutaishan), and Monju reverrence in Japan is centered around Mt. Godai. Monju Crossing the Sea is a favorite theme that depicts Monju riding a lion and accompanied by Zenzai Doji and three other young attendants. Monju is also reverrenced as a kitchen or dining area deity. In that role he takes the form of a Buddhist priest.

Fugen frequently appears with Monju as an attendant to Shaka. While Monju rides a lion, Fugen rides a white elephant. Fugen particularly helps females attain enlightenment, and for that reason is popular among females of all ages.

Nikko and Gakko: Nikko and Gakko are bodhisattva attendants to Yakushi Nyorai. Nikko has a sun shape in his crown: Gakko has a moon shape. Nikko and Gakko images will also sometimes carry sun and moon shaped implements.

Jizo: During the 56 billion 70 million years between Buddha's demise and Miroku's second descent, Jizo Bosatsu is on Earth to help men toward salvation. Men are subject to six types of maya – called the *rokudo* (six ways) in Japanese – that prevent them from reaching enlightenment. Jizo is known for being able to save even those souls suffering in Hell, one of the *rokudo*. Jizo is thus sometimes called Rokudo (Rikido) Jizo. A more familiar Jizo form is the Jizo of Longevity, which holds a short crosier and a wondrous jewel.

Kokuzo: *Kokuzo* means "accomplishments and virtues as vast and boundless as the heavens." The Kokuzo Bosatsu image in Gakuan-ji Temple (photo 72) is a memorial to the priest Doji (? – 744) who visited T'ang China from 701 to 718 and brought to Japan Buddhist teachings that were influential during the Nara Period. The five great Kokuzo are five forms of Gochi Dainichi Butsu: Goyu, Kongo, Hokai, Hoko, and Renge.

Fudo Myoo: Shiva, an important deity in Hinduism, is said to have been carried directly into Buddhism as Fudo Myoo. Originally he was considered a messenger for Dainichi Nyorai. Together with the spread of esoteric Buddhism, however, Fudo Myoo gradually was looked upon not as a mere messenger but as a transformed Dainichi Nyorai. As with other Myoo, Fudo Myoo wears only a short robe from the waist down. He presents a fearful appearance with his hair shooting out like flames, and his canine teeth bared. He holds a sword or some other weapon, and decorates his body with snake or bone accessories.

Fudo carries a sword in his right hand and a snaring rope in his left. His hair usually falls down over his left shoulder, and he sits on a stone pedestal with a flame-like halo behind him. Fudo Myoo in the very early Heian Period, like the image in To-ji Temples's Lecture Hall (photo 74) has both eyes open and either the upper or lower canine teeth bared. Later in Heian, as with Fudo in Sangatsudo Hall of Todai-ji Temple (photo 73), many Fudo images have one yee open and the other half-open, as if glaring, and the canine teeth are bared one downward from the upper teeth, and one upward from the lower teeth. Fudo Myoo's sword gradually acquired a coiled *naga* (an imaginary water serpent) decoration. This *kurikara* sword eventually came to symbolize Fudo. The Eight Great

Child Servants, particularly Kongara and Seitaka, often accompany Fudo.

Godai Myoo: The Godai Myoo are mutation of Gochi Dainichi Nyorai. Fudo Myoo is the central figure and is surrounded by Gozanze (East), Gundari (South), Daiitoku (West), and Kongo Yasha (North). Each Myoo is backed by a flaming halo, stands on either a rock or devil pedestal, wears the Myoo's fearful expression, and brandishes various weapons.

Other Myoo include Bato, Dairin, Munosho, Daigensui, Aizen, and Kujaku. Akishino-dera Temple is called the birthplace of Oguru Sujogyo, the man who played a leading role in bringing the first Daigensui image to Japan. The Daigensui image in Akishino-dera dates from the Kamakura Period. It is opened for public viewing only once a year.

Aizen Myoo has the power to turn man's lustful passions into pure love. He carries a bow and arrow, and is backed by a red sun corona. He usually has four or six arms. Aizen images may be viewed in Saidai-ji Temple (photo 75), in Kongobu-ji Temple on Mt. Koya, in Jingo-ji Temple, and elsewhere.

Bon Ten and Taishaku Ten: Ten, like Myoo, are deities borrowed from Hinduism. They serve as guardian deities for Buddhism. Among Ten, Bon and Taishaku serve in the highest positions, very close to Shaka. They protect the principal images in Horyu-ji Temple's Hozoden Treasury (photo 89), Todai-ji Temple's Sangatsudo Hall (photo 88), and Kondo Hall in Toshodai-ji Temple (photo 90). All these Bon and Taishaku images wear Chinese style garments under which a careful viewer will glimpse the armor that marks them as guardians of the religion.

In esoteric Buddhism, Bon and Taishaku Ten acquired central importance among the twelve great Ten. Taishaku frequently rides a white elephant, while Bon Ten rides three geese.

Shi Tenno (Four Deva): The Shi Tenno are deities guarding the gates to Buddhism in four directions. They entered Japan together with Buddhism, and often appear standing at the four corners of platforms on which Nyorai and Bodhisattva stand. Tamon stands guarding the north, Jikoku the east, Komoku the west, and Zocho the south. Since the Shi Tenno acutally stand at the corners of the platforms, each is forty-five degrees away from the true direction. In short, Tamon stands nortneast, Jikoku southeast, Komoku southwest, and Zocho northwest.

Shi Tenno, serving as protectors of the religion must subdue all transgressors. To symbolize this role, the Shi Tenno are shown standing on evil beasts. The Asuka Period Shi Tenno in Horyu-ji Temple's Kondo Hall (photo 82) stand quietly on four beasts that raise no particular fuss. The beasts seem to serve merely as pedestals. In the Hakuho Period, represented by images in Kondo Hall of Taima-dera Temple (photo 83), the Shi Tenno begin to show movement, although at first it is restricted to hand movements. In the Nara and Heian Periods, movement becomes more pronounced – in the beasts as well as the Shi Tenno images. Examples are the Nara Period sculptures in Kaidanin (photo 84) and Sangatsudo Hall (Photo 85) of Todai-ji Temple, and the Heian Period sculptures in the Lecture Hall of To-ji Temple (photo 86).

Sometime after the Heian Period, Tamon Ten was separated from the other Ten and became reverred as Bishamon Ten. He later became popularized as one of the Seven Deities of Good Fortune. Tobatsu Bishamon Ten (photo 87) is another form of Tamon. He wears the dress of Tobatsu, one of the lands west of China.

Nio (Kongo Rikishi): Nio are two forms of Taishaku Ten, and stand guard at temple gates. When Taishaku stands in a single transformation, the image is Shukongoshin (photo 96). The oldest Nio images in Japan are those at Chumon Gate (photo 93) of Horyu-ji Temple. The largest wooden images are at Todai-ji Temple's Nandaimon Gate (photo 95). The most realistic looking are the Kamakura Period works in the Treasury (photo 93) of Kofuku-ji Templ^ Nio usuallv appear one with his mouth open, as if roaring in anger, and the other with his mouth closed. The mouth open/mouth closed contrast emphasizes the fact that the two were originally one. In other words, a single body can have its mouth open at one time and closed at another. Two open or two closed mouths would suggest two bodies.

Hachibushu: The Hachibushu are deities of foreign religions, formerly kings of birds and beasts. Shaka converted them and they became protectors of Buddhism. Together with the Ten Great Disciples, the Hachibushu form a group that frequently surrounds Shaka Nyorai. Kofuku-ji Temple boasts of highly realistic dry lacquer Hachibushu images dating from the Nara Period. The three-faced, six-armed Ashura (photo 97) in that group is popular among lovers of old sculpture.

Juni Jinsho: These are twelve generals who guard the twelve sacred vows of Yakushi Nyorai. They stand close to Yakushi and thus appear frequently with Nikko and Gakko Bodhisattva. The twelve generals stand watch an hour each in day and at night. They later were associated with the twelve Chinese zodiacal signs, and each general came to bear its particular sign engraved on its crown.

The Yakushi Nyorai image in Shin Yakushi-ji Temple's Main Hall (photo 99) is a wooden Heian Period production while eleven of the twelve protector generals are stucco images of the Nara Period. The Basara Daisho image deserves special mention. Since the twelve Jinsho surround Yakushi, they usually are smaller than the average Buddhist image.

Female Ten: Fearful males are not the only Ten. As related earlier, some Ten are beautiful, voluptuous females. Four of the best-known female Ten are Kissho, Benzai, Gigei, and Kariteibo. Kissho reverence began in the Nara Period, and records dated 767 exist that mention a religious ceremony surrounding Kissho. The Kissho image (photo 103) in Todai-ji Temple's Sangatsudo Hall is a life-size product of the Nara Period. One easily imagines Buddhist memorial services being held with this as the principal image. The beautiful colorings used in the Kamakura Period Kissho Ten (photo 101) in the Main Hall of Joruri-ji Temple, and the rich, deep expression of the Nara Period Gigei Ten (photo 100) in the Main Hall of Akishino-dera Temple give these female Ten images special prominence among Japan's Buddhist sculptures.

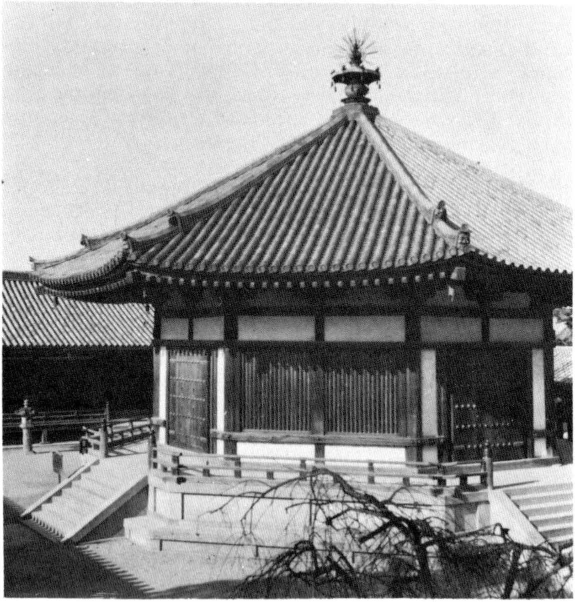

Yume-dono (Horyu-ji Temple)

GLOSSARY

Aizen Myoo（愛染明王）: Ragaraja
Amida Nyorai（阿弥陀如来）: Amitabha
Anchira Taisho（安底羅）: Andira
Basara Taisho（伐折羅）: Vajra
Bato Kannon（馬頭観音）: Hayagriva
Benzai Ten（弁才天）: Sarasvati
Bishamon Ten（毘沙門天）: Vaisrovana
Bon Ten（梵天）: Brahman
Bosatsu（菩薩）: bodhisattva, one who chooses through compassionate zeal to remain in the wheel of existence to aid fellow men toward salvation
Daigensui Myoo（大元帥明王）: Atavaka
Daiitoku Myoo（大威徳明王）: Yamantaka
Dainichi Nyorai（大日如来）: Mahavairocana (see also Rushana)
Dennyoirin Kannon（伝如意輪観音）: see Nyoirin Kannon
Fudo Myoo（不動明王）: Acalanatha (see also Godai Myoo)
Fugen Bosatsu（普賢菩薩）: Samantabhadra
Fuku Kenjaku Kannon（不空羂索観音）: Amoghapasa
Gakko Bosatsu（月光菩薩）: Candraprabha
Gigei Ten（伎芸天）: Mahesvara
Godai Myoo（五大明王）: Five Great Myoo (Gozanze, Daiitoku, Gundari, Kongo Yasha, and Fudo)
Godai Kokuzo（五大虚空蔵）: Five Great Kokuzo, five forms of Akasagarbha

Goyu – North　　Hoko – South
Kongo – East　　Renge – West
Hokai – Central

Gozanze Myoo（降三世明王）: Trailokyavijaya
Gundari Myoo（軍荼利明王）: Kundali (see also Godai Myoo)
Guze Kannon（救世観音）: see Shokannon

Hachibushu（八部衆）: Eight protectors of Buddha

Ten : Deva	Ashura – Asura
Ryuo – Naga	Karura – Garuda
Yasha – Yaksa	Magoraka – Mahoraga
Kendatsuba – Gandharva	Kinnara – Kimnara

Jikoku Ten（持国天）: Dhrtarastra

Jizo Bosatsu（地蔵菩薩）: Ksitigarbha

Juichimen Kannon（十一面観音）: Ekadasamukha, Eleven-face Kannon

(small heads on Kannon's crown; three faces of mercy on front, three of anger to left, three baring fangs upward to right, one laughing, and one of Amida)

Juni Jinsho（十二神将）: Twelve Generals

Kumbhira	Indra
Vajra	Pajra
Mihira	Makura
Andira	Sindura
Majira	Catura
Sandira	Vikarala

Juni Ten（十二天）: Twelve Deva Guardians

Taishaku (Indira)	East
Ka (Agri)	Southeast
Enma (Yama)	South
Rasetsu (Raksasa)	Southwest
Sui (Varuna)	West
Fu (Vayu)	Northwest
Bishamon (Vaisravana)	North
Ishana (Isana)	Northeast
Bon (Brahman)	Heaven
Ji (Prthivi)	Earth
Nitten (Surya, Aditya)	Sun
Gatten (Candra)	Moon

Juntei Kannon （准胝観音）: Cundi
Kannon Bosatsu （観音菩薩）: see Shokannon
Kissho Ten （吉祥天）: Mahasri
Kokuzo Bosatsu （虚空蔵菩薩）: Akasagarbha
Komoku Ten （広目天）: see Shi Tenno
Kongo Rikishi （金剛力士）: see Nio
Miroku Bosatsu （弥勒菩薩）: Maitreya
Monju Bosatsu （文殊菩薩）: Majusri
Myoo （明王）: see Godai Myoo
Nikko Bosatsu （日光菩薩）: Suryaprabha
Nio （仁王）: Vajradhara
Nyoirin Kannon （如意輪観音）: Cintamanicakra
Rushana （盧遮那）: Vairocana (see also Dainichi Nyorai)
Senju Kannon （千手観音）: Sahasrabhuja
Shaka Nyorai （釈迦如来）: Sakyamuni
Shi Tenno （四天王）: Four Heavenly Kings, Guardians of Four Directions in Land of Buddha

Tamon (Vaisrovana)	North
Jikoku (Dhrtarastra)	East
Komoku (Virupaksa)	West
Zocho (Virudhaka)	South

Shokannon （聖観音）: Avalokitesvara
Shukongoshin （執金剛神）: see Nio
Taishaku Ten （帝釈天）: see Juni Ten
Tanjo Shaka （誕生釈迦）: Sakyamuni at birth
Tobatsu Bishamon Ten （兜跋毘沙門天）: see Bishamon Ten
Yakushi Nyorai （薬師如来）: Bhaisajya-guru
Yoryu Kannon （楊柳観音）: Avalokitesvara with willow branch
Zenzai Doji （善財童子）: child attendant to Fugen
Zocho Ten （増長天）: see Shi Tenno

Temples in this book

Akishino-dera (秋篠寺) Akishino, Akishino-cho, Nara City
Asuka-ji (飛鳥寺) Asuka-mura, Takaichi-gun, Nara Pref.
Byodo-in (平等院) Renge, Uji-cho, Uji City
Chugu-ji (中宮寺) Ikaruga-cho, Ikoma-gun, Nara Pref.
Daian-ji (大安寺) Daianji-cho, Nara City
Domyo-ji (道明寺) Domyoji-cho, Minamikawachi-gun, Osaka Pref.
Enjo-ji (円成寺) Ninnikusen-cho, Nara City
Fujii-dera (藤井寺) Fujiidera-cho, Minamikawachi-gun, Osaka Pref.
Fukuchi-in (福智院) Fukuchiin-cho, Nara City
Gakuan-ji (額安寺) Nukatabe, Yamatokoriyama City
Genko-ji (元興寺) Shibashinya-cho, Nara City
Genko-ji Gokuraku-bo (元興寺極楽坊) Chuin-cho, Nara City
Hannya-ji (般若寺) Hannyaji-cho, Nara City
Hokai-ji (法界寺) Daigo, Fushimi-ku, Kyoto City
Hokke-ji (法華寺) Hokkeji-cho, Nara City
Horin-ji (法輪寺) Ikaruga-cho, Ikoma-gun, Nara Pref.
Horyu-ji (法隆寺) Ikaruga-cho, Ikoma-gun, Nara Pref.
Jingo-ji (神護寺) Takao-cho, Umegahata, Ukyo-ku, Kyoto City
Joruri-ji (浄瑠璃寺) Kamo-cho, Soraku-gun, Kyoto Pref.
Jurin-in (十輪院) Jurinin-cho, Nara City
Kaniman-ji (蟹満寺) Yamashiro-cho, Soraku-gun, Kyoto Pref.
Kannon-ji (観音寺) Fukenji, Tanabe-cho, Tsuzuki-gun, Kyoto Pref.
Kanshin-ji (観心寺) Teramoto, Kawachinagano City
Kofuku-ji (興福寺) Noborioji-cho, Nara City
Koryu-ji (広隆寺) Hachioka-cho, Uzumasa, Kyoto City
Monju-in (文殊院) Abe, Sakurai-shi, Nara Pref.
Muro-ji (室生寺) Muro-mura, Uda-gun, Nara Pref.
Oka-dera (岡寺) Oka, Asuka-mura, Takaichi-gun, Nara Pref.
Saidai-ji (西大寺) Saidaiji-cho, Nara City
Shinyakushi-ji (新薬師寺) Takahata-cho, Nara City
Shorin-ji (聖林寺) Shimo, Sakurai-shi, Nara Pref.
Taima-dera (当麻寺) Taima-mura, Kitakatsuragi-gun, Nara Pref.
Todai-ji (東大寺) Zoshi-cho, Nara City
To-ji (東寺) Kujo-cho, Minami-ku, Kyoto City
Toshodai-ji (唐招提寺) Gojo-cho, Nara City
Yakushi-ji (薬師寺) Nishinokyo, Nara City

HOIKUSHA COLOR BOOKS

ENGLISH EDITIONS

Book Size 4″×6″

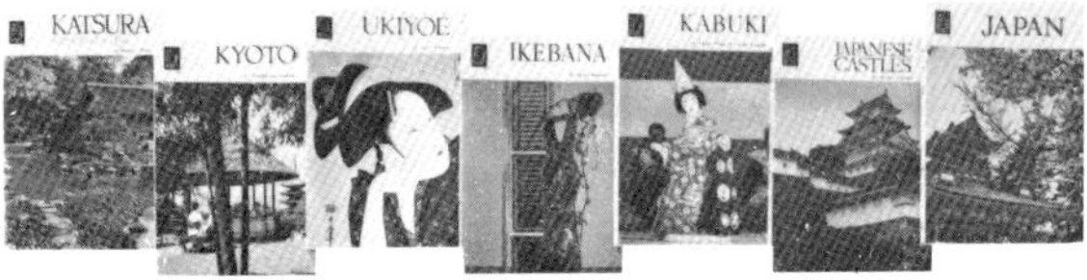

① KATSURA
② TOKAIDO Hiroshige
③ EMAKI
④ KYOTO
⑤ UKIYOE
⑥ GEM STONES
⑦ NARA
⑧ TOKYO Past and Present
⑨ KYOTO GARDENS
⑩ IKEBANA
⑪ KABUKI
⑫ JAPANESE CASTLES
⑬ JAPANESE FESTIVALS
⑭ WOOD-BLOCK PRINTING
⑮ N O H
⑯ HAWAII
⑰ JAPAN
⑱ BUDDHIST IMAGES
⑲ OSAKA
⑳ HOKUSAI
㉑ ORIGAMI
㉒ JAPANESE SWORDS
㉓ GOLDFISH
㉔ SUMI-E
㉕ SHELLS OF JAPAN
㉖ FOLK ART
㉗ TOKYO NIKKO FUJI
㉘ NATIONAL FLAGS
㉙ BONSAI
㉚ UTAMARO
㉛ TEA CEREMONY
㉜ PAPER DOLLS
㉝ JAPANESE CERAMICS
㉞ MODEL CARS
㉟ CREATIVE ORIGAMI
㊱ Z E N
㊲ KIMONO
㊳ CHINESE COOKING
㊴ KYOGEN
㊵ NOH MASKS
㊶ LIVING ORIGAMI
㊷ SHINKANSEN
㊸ OSAKA CASTLE
㊹ BUNRAKU

COLORED ILLUSTRATIONS FOR NATURALISTS

Text in Japanese, with index in Latin or English.

Book Size 6″ × 8″

1. BUTTERFLIES of JAPAN
2. INSECTS of JAPAN vol.1
3. INSECTS of JAPAN vol.2
4. SHELLS of JAPAN vol.1
5. FISHES of JAPAN vol.1
6. BIRDS of JAPAN
7. MAMMALS of JAPAN
8. SEA SHORE ANIMALS of JAPAN
9. GARDEN FLOWERS vol.1
10. GARDEN FLOWERS vol.2
11. ROSES and ORCHIDS
12. ALPINE FLORA of JAPAN vol.1
13. ROCKS
14. ECONOMIC MINERALS
15. HERBACEOUS PLANTS of JAPAN vol.1
16. HERBACEOUS PLANTS of JAPAN vol.2
17. HERBACEOUS PLANTS of JAPAN vol.3
18. SEAWEEDS of JAPAN
19. TREES and SHRUBS of JAPAN
20. EXOTIC AQUARIUM FISHES vol.1
21. MOTHS of JAPAN vol.1
22. MOTHS of JAPAN vol.2
23. FUNGI of JAPAN vol.1
24. PTERIDOPHYTA of JAPAN
25. SHELLS of JAPAN vol.2
26. FISHES of JAPAN vol.2
27. EXOTIC AQUARIUM FISHES vol.2
28. ALPINE FLORA of JAPAN vol.2
29. FRUITS
30. REPTILES and AMPHIBIANS of JAPAN
31. ECONOMIC MINERALS vol.2
32. FRESHWATER FISHES of JAPAN
33. GARDEN PLANTS of the WORLD vol.1
34. GARDEN PLANTS of the WORLD vol.2
35. GARDEN PLANTS of the WORLD vol.3
36. GARDEN PLANTS of the WORLD vol.4
37. GARDEN PLANTS of the WORLD vol.5
38. THE FRESHWATER PLANKTON of JAPAN
39. MEDICINAL PLANTS of JAPAN

40. VEGETABLE CROPS of JAPAN
41. FARM ANIMALS of JAPAN
42. FUNGI of JAPAN vol.2
43. SHELLS of the WORLD vol.1
44. SHELLS of the WORLD vol.2
45. THE MARINE PLANKTON of JAPAN
46. EARLY STAGES of JAPANESE MOTHS vol.1
47. EARLY STAGES of JAPANESE MOTHS vol.2
48. FOSSILS
49. WOODY PLANTS of JAPAN vol.1
50. WOODY PLANTS of JAPAN vol.2
51. BRYOPHYTES of JAPAN
52. LICHEN FLORA of JAPAN
53. NATURALIZED PLANTS of JAPAN
54. DISEASES and PESTS of CULTIVATED TREES and SHRUBS
55. DISEASES and PESTS of FLOWERS and VEGETABLES
56. WAKAN-YAKU vol.1
57. WAKAN-YAKU vol.2
58. Coloured Guide of Wild Herbs with Artificial Key to Their Families
59. THE NEW ALPINE FLORA of JAPAN vol. I
60. THE NEW ALPINE FLORA of JAPAN vol. II
61. THE LAND SNAILS of JAPAN
62. JAPANESE CRUSTACEAN DECAPODS and STOMATOPODS vol. I
63. JAPANESE CRUSTACEAN DECAPODS and STOMATOPODS vol. II
64. THE LIFE HISTORIES OF BUTTERFLIES IN JAPAN vol. I
65. THE LIFE HISTORIES OF BUTTERFLIES IN JAPAN vol. II
66. THE LIFE HISTORIES OF BUTTERFLIES IN JAPAN vol. III
67. THE LIFE HISTORIES OF BUTTERFLIES IN JAPAN vol. IV
68. THE COLEOPTERA OF JAPAN vol. I
69. THE COLEOPTERA OF JAPAN vol. II
70. THE COLEOPTERA OF JAPAN vol. III
71. THE COLEOPTERA OF JAPAN vol. IV
72. Colored Illustrations of The Marine Fishes of Japan Vol. I
73. Colored Illustrations of The Marine Fishes of Japan Vol. II
74. SPIDERS OF JAPAN IN COLOR
75. Colored Illustrations of Mushrooms of Japan Vol. I
76. Colored Illustrations of Mushrooms of Japan Vol. II
77. Ornamental Tropical Plants of the World Vol. I

<ENGLISH EDITIONS>

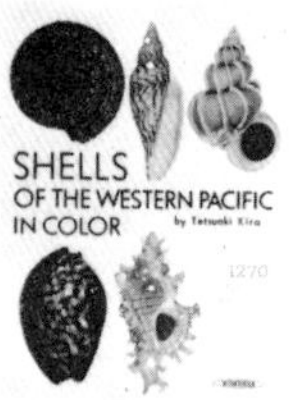

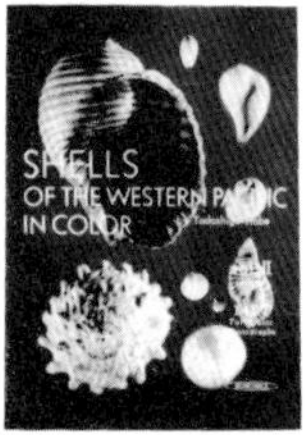

SHELLS OF THE WESTERN PACIFIC IN COLOR

Book Size 7″×10″

〈vol. I〉 by Tetsuaki Kira
(304 pages, 72 in color)
〈vol. II〉 by Tadashige Habe
(304 pages, 66 in color)

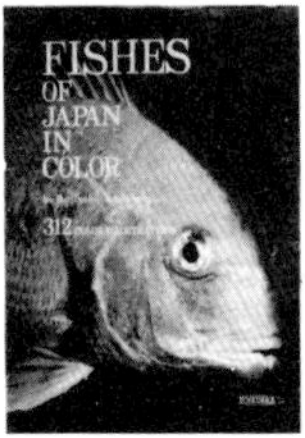

FISHES OF JAPAN IN COLOR

Book Size 7″×10″

by Toshiji Kamohara
(210 pages, 64 in color)